THIS BOOK BELONGS TO:

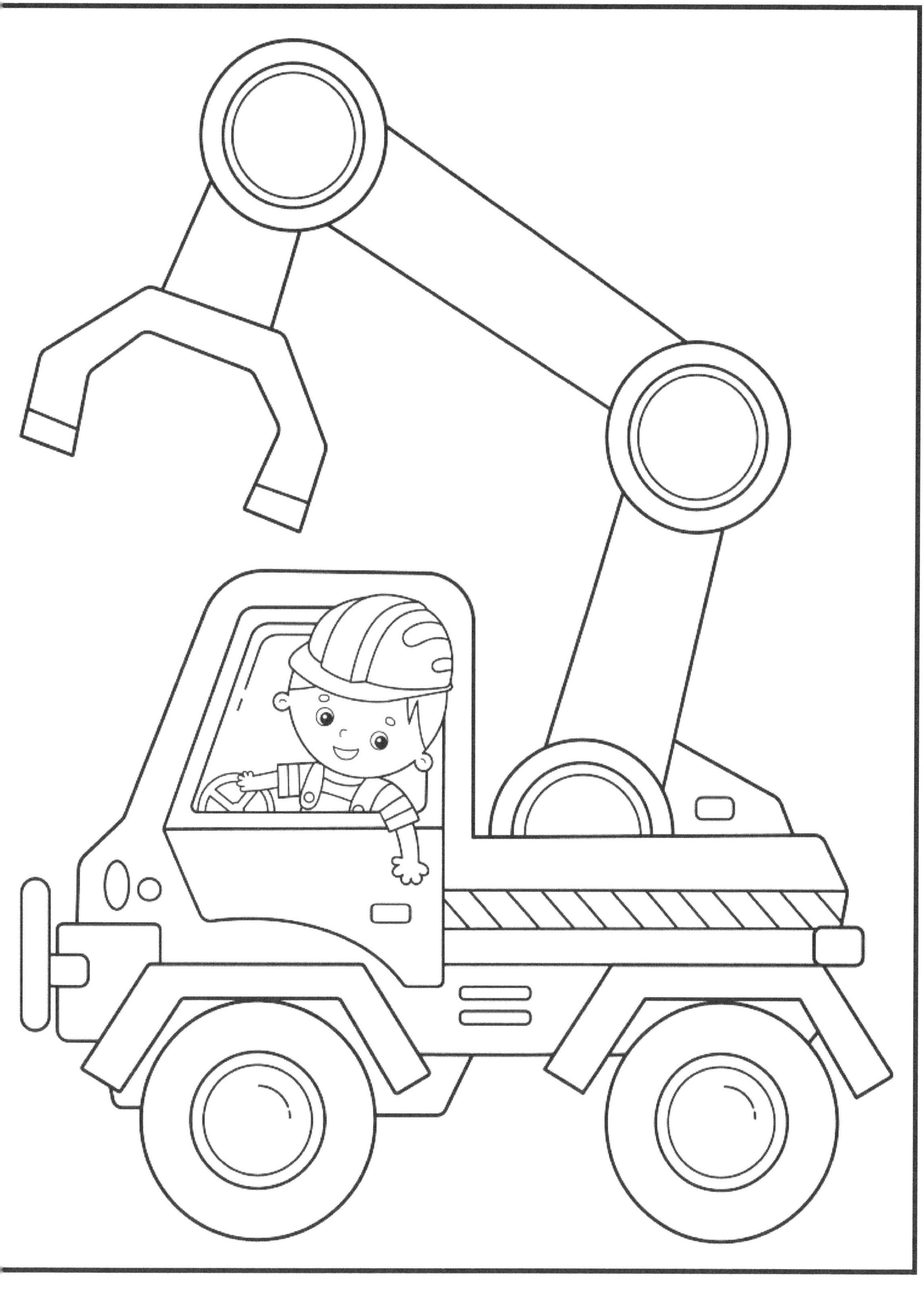

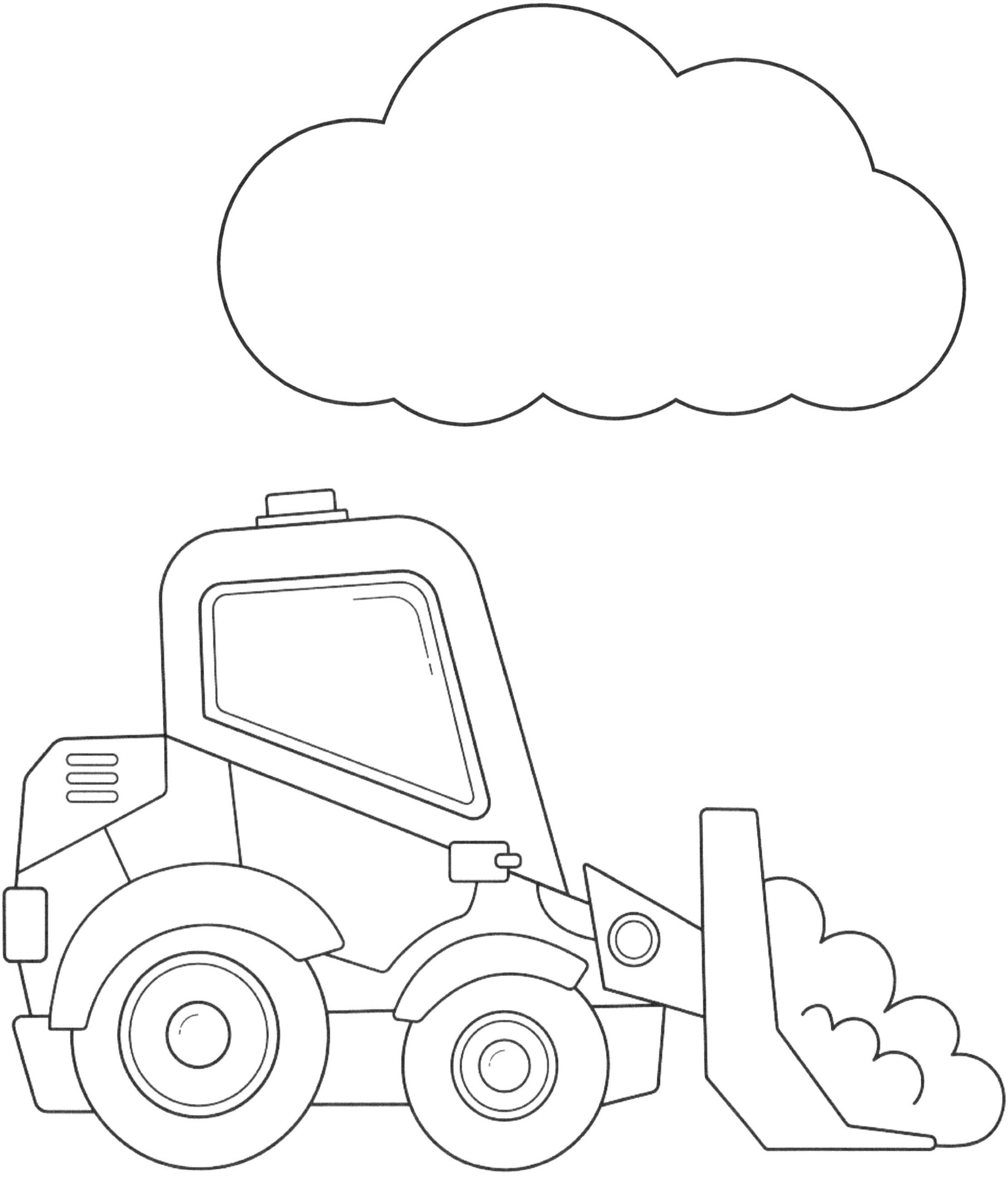

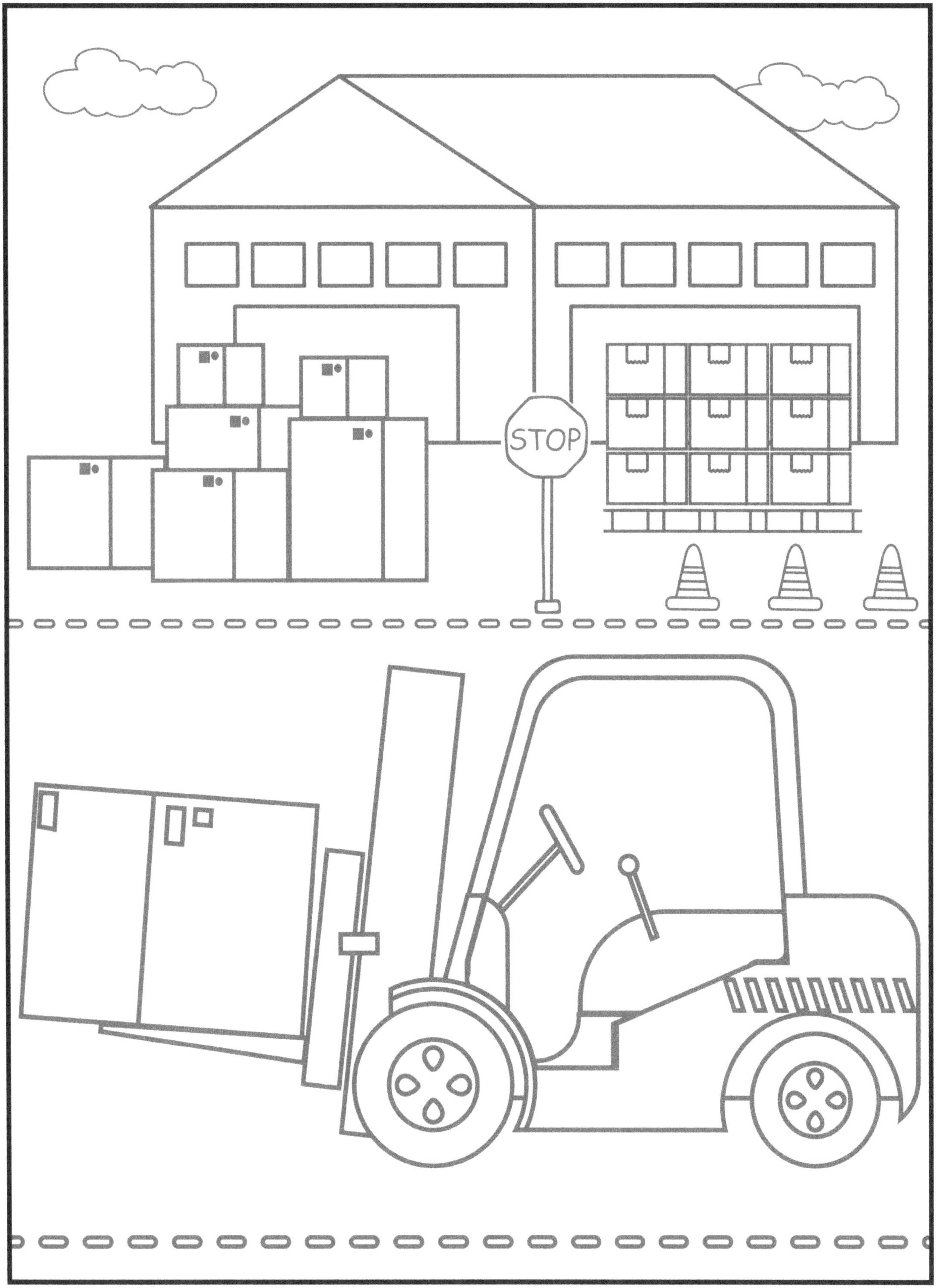
STOP

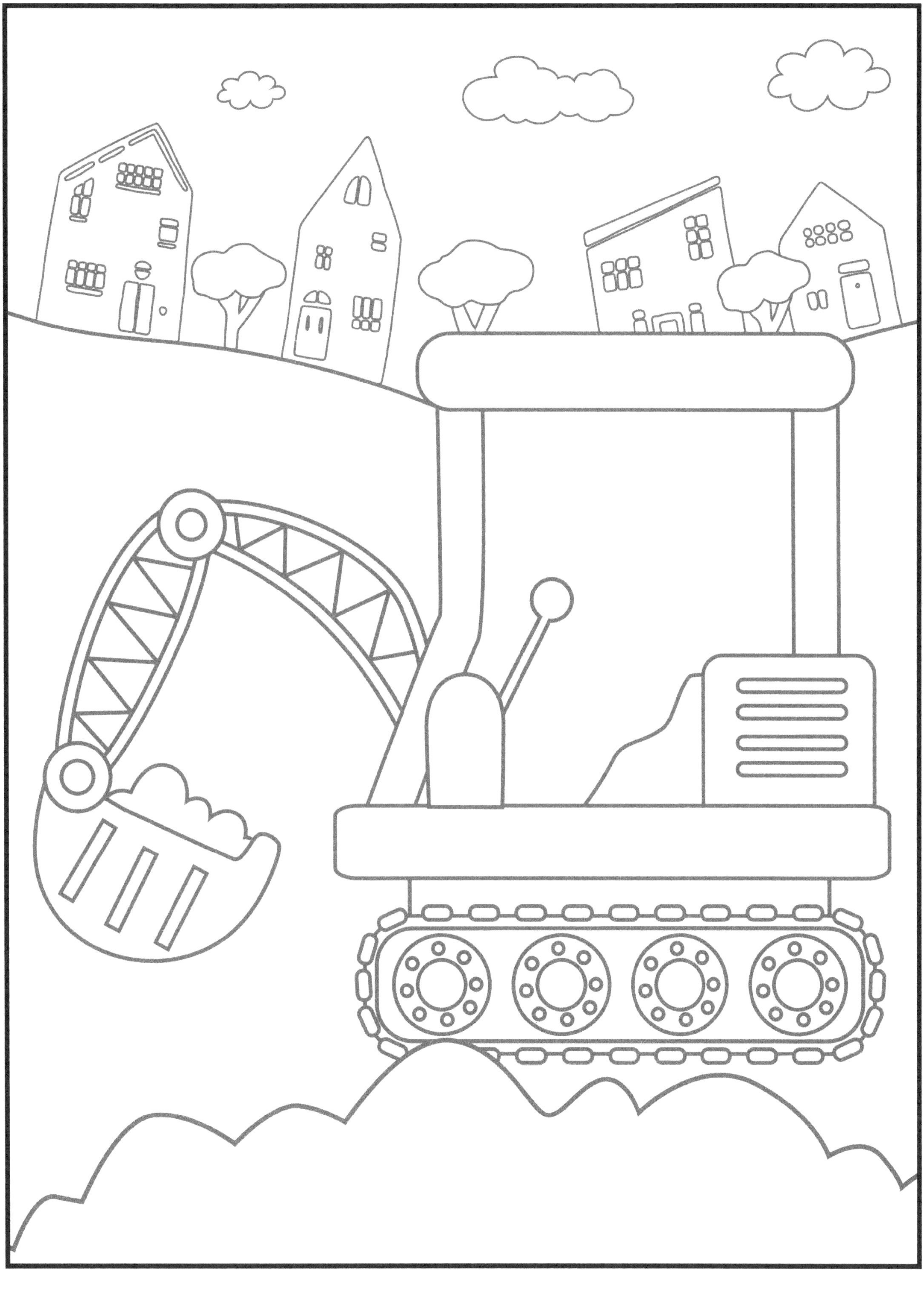

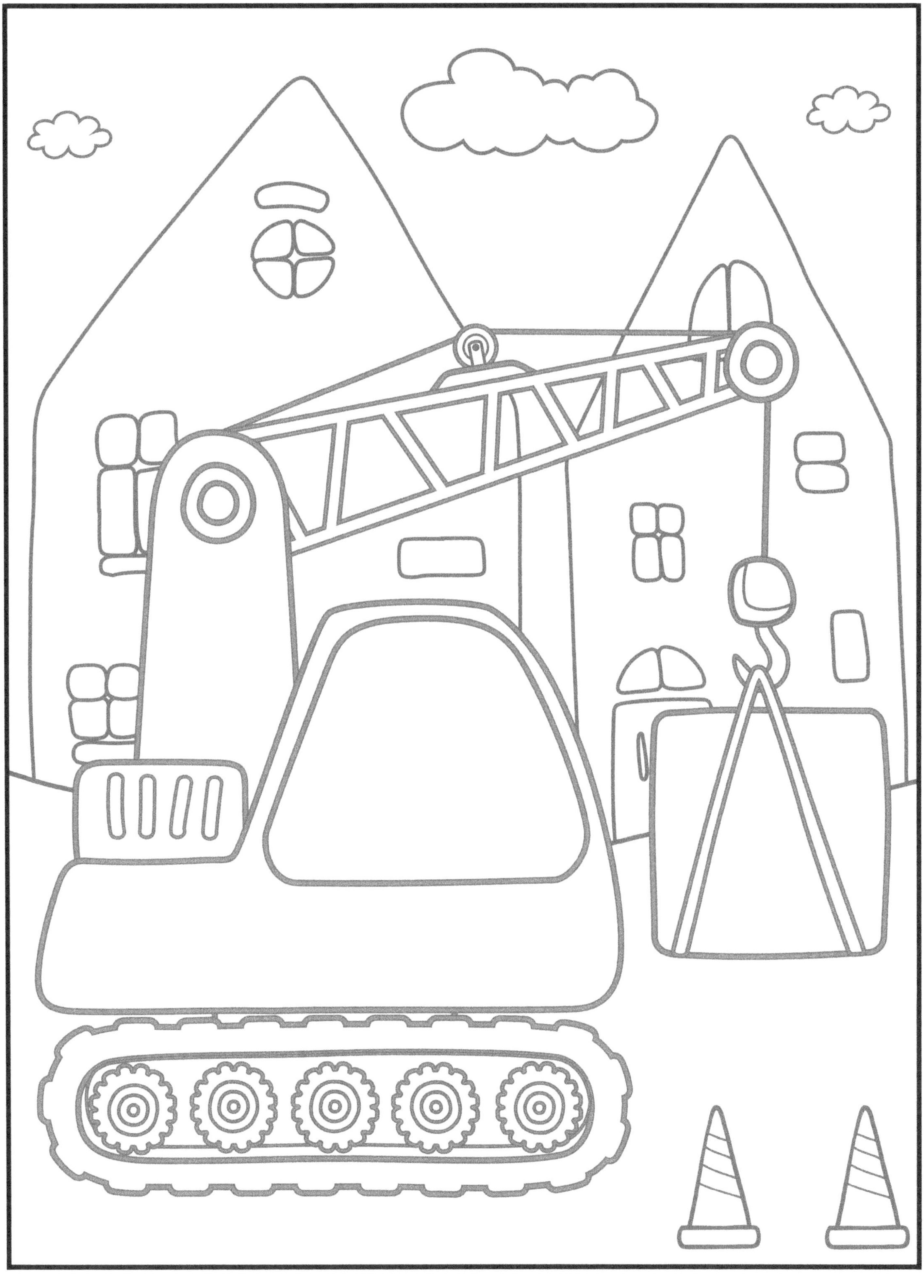

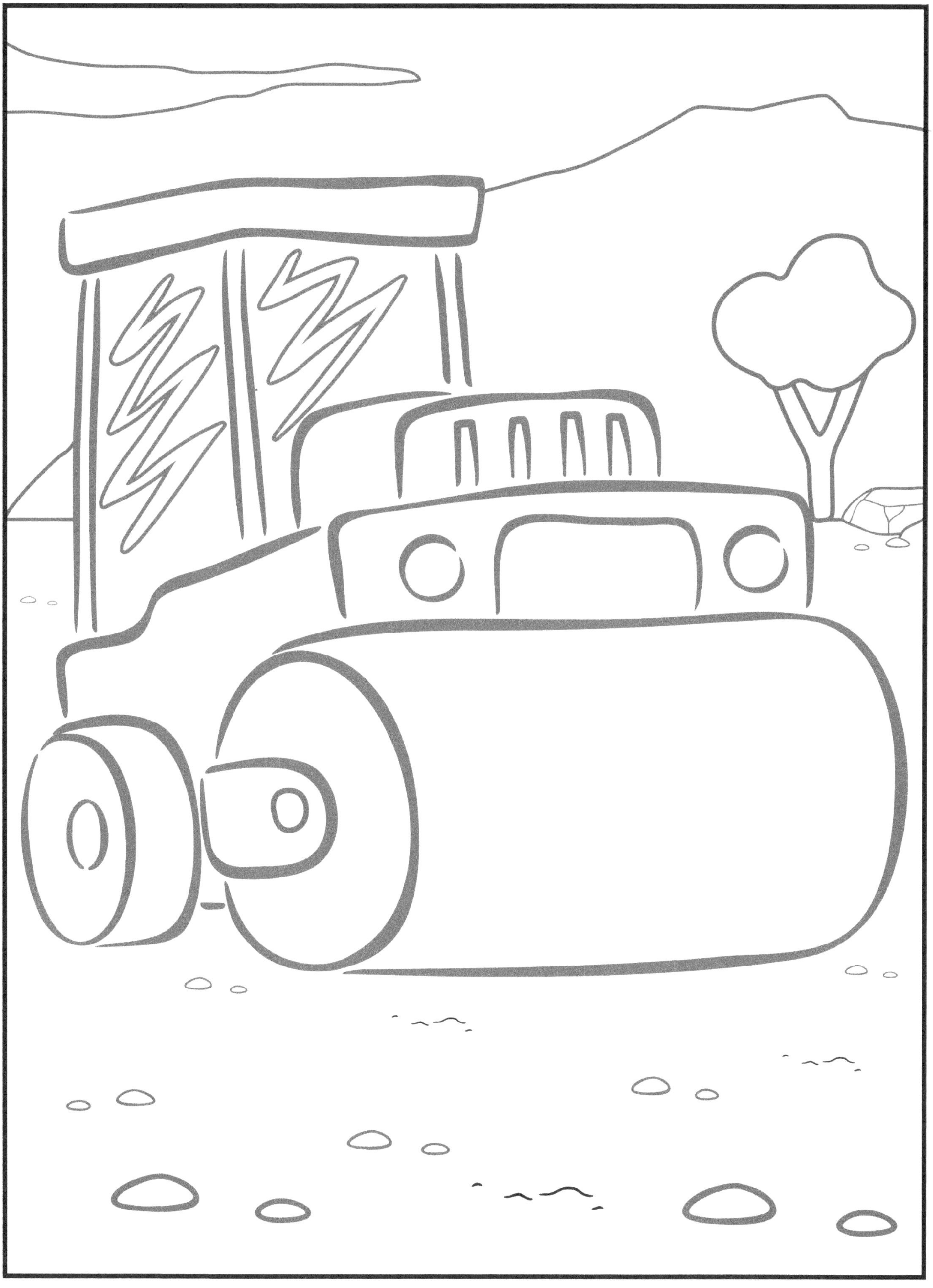

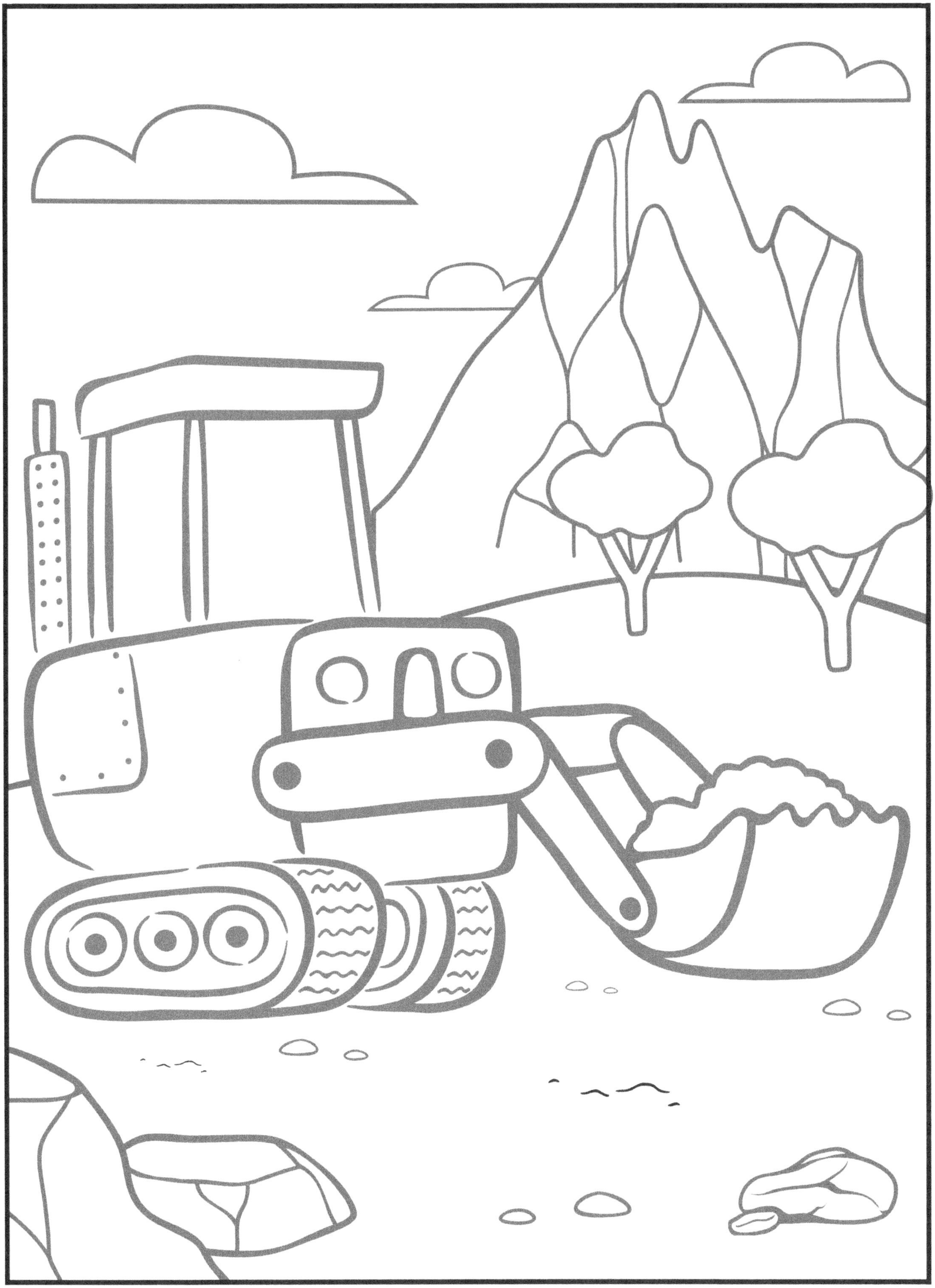

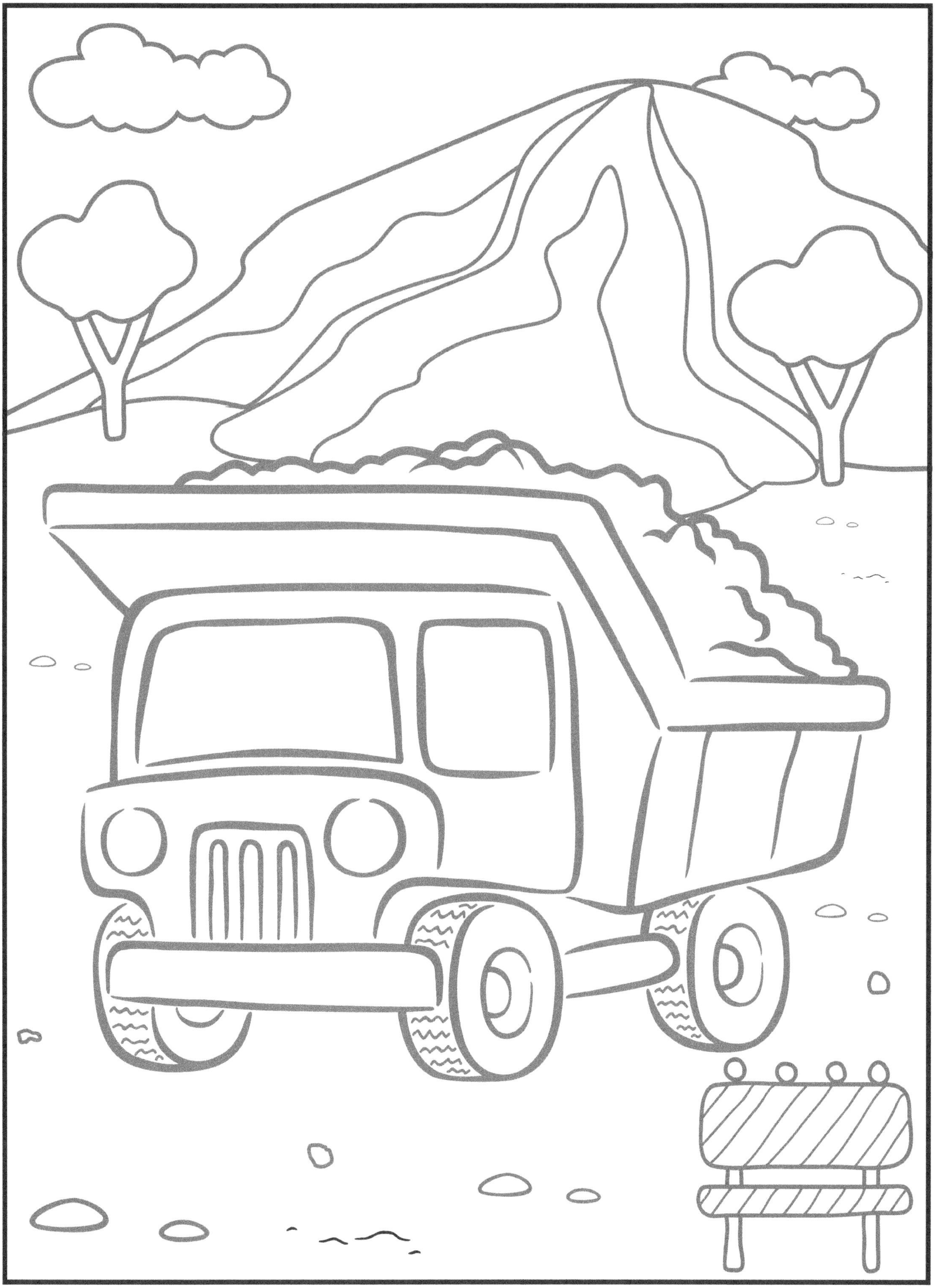

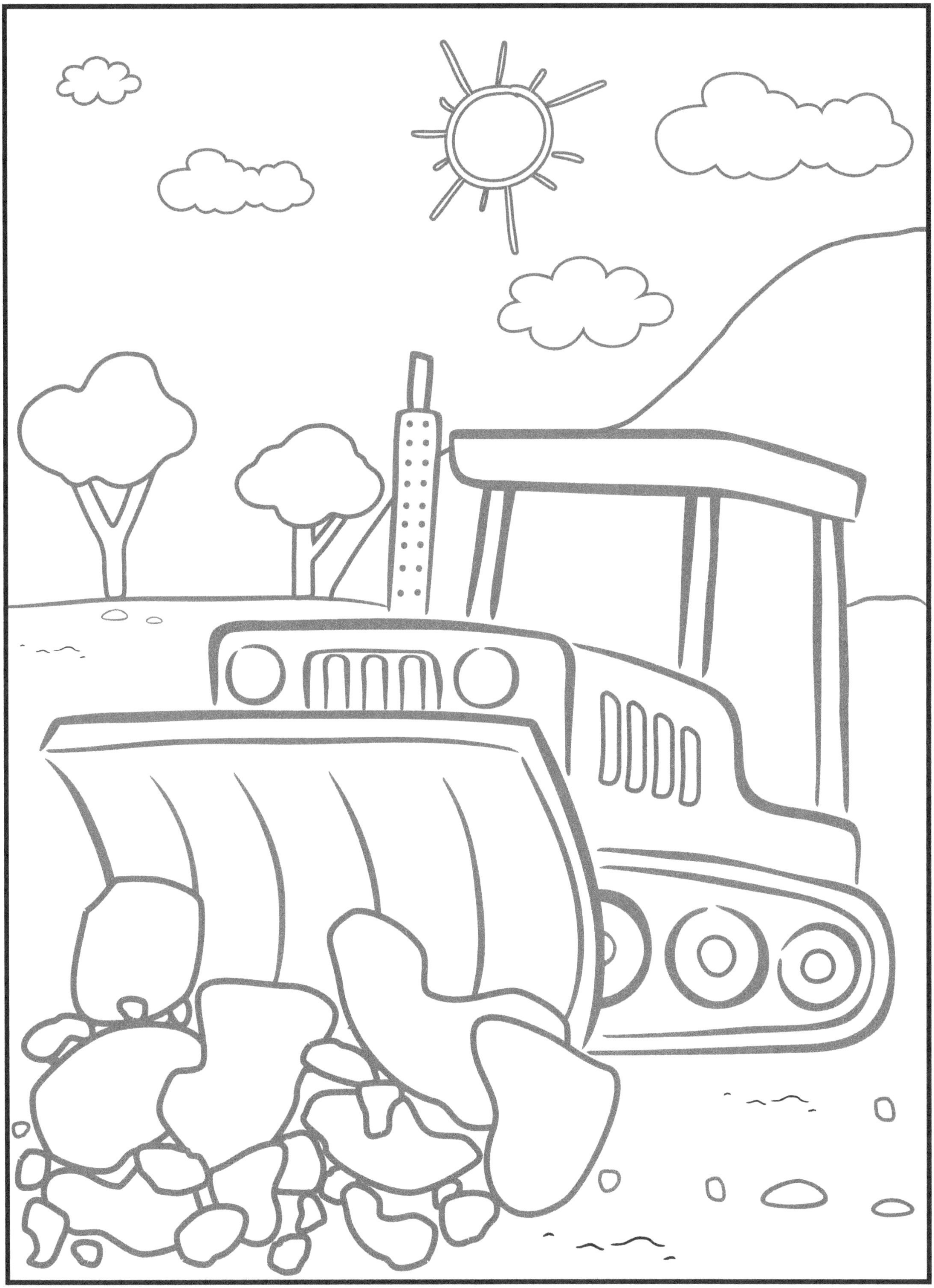

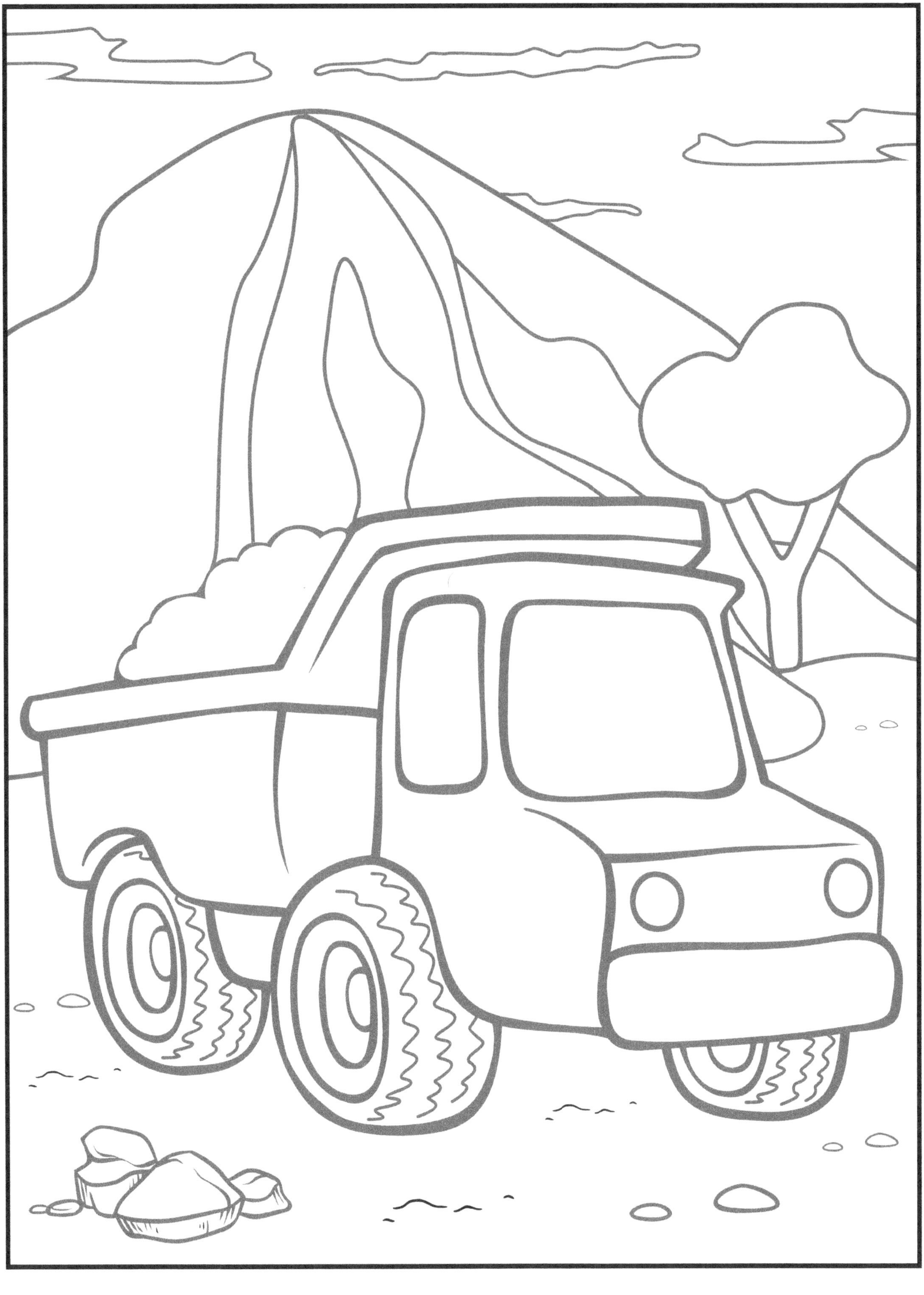

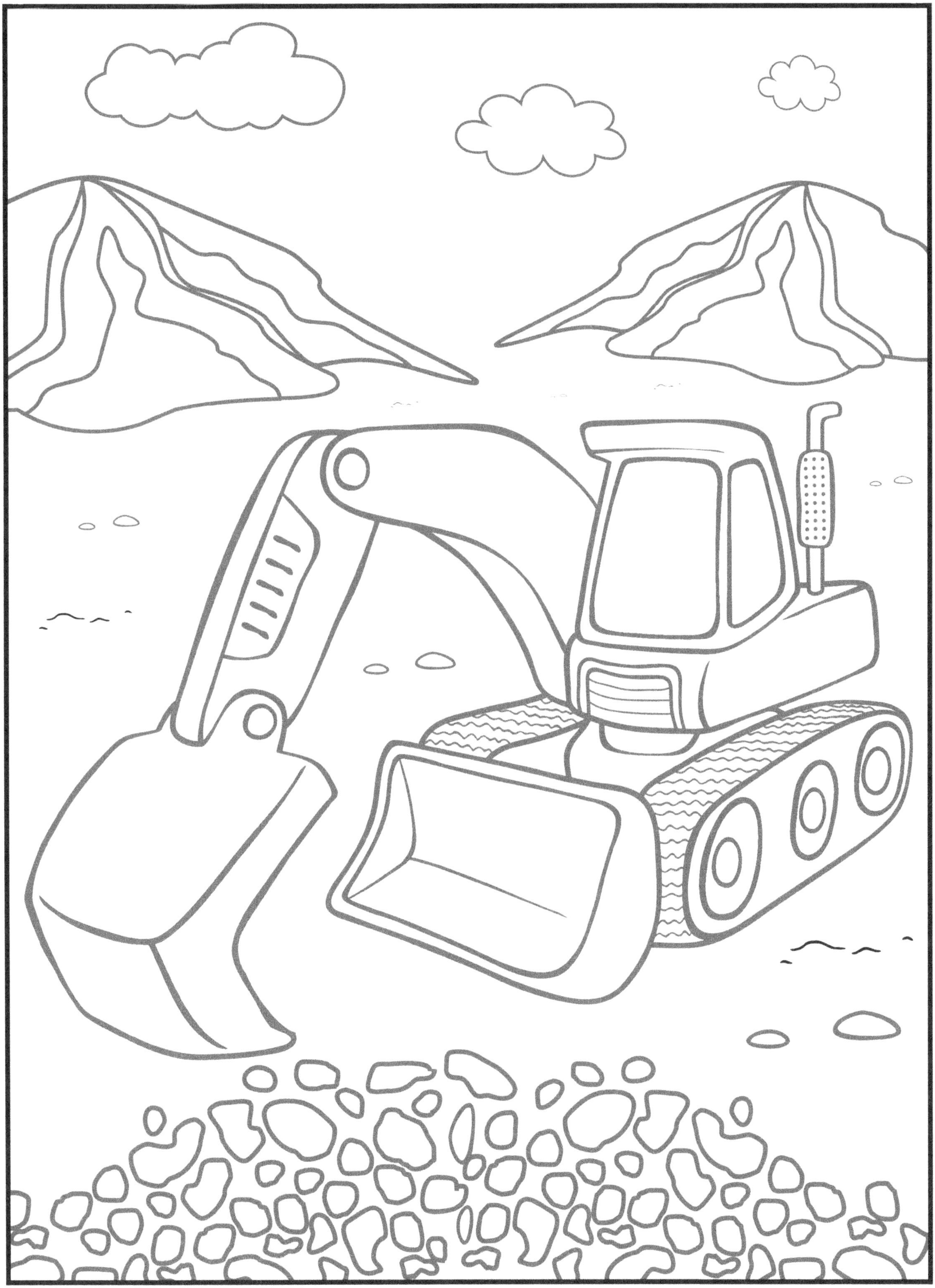

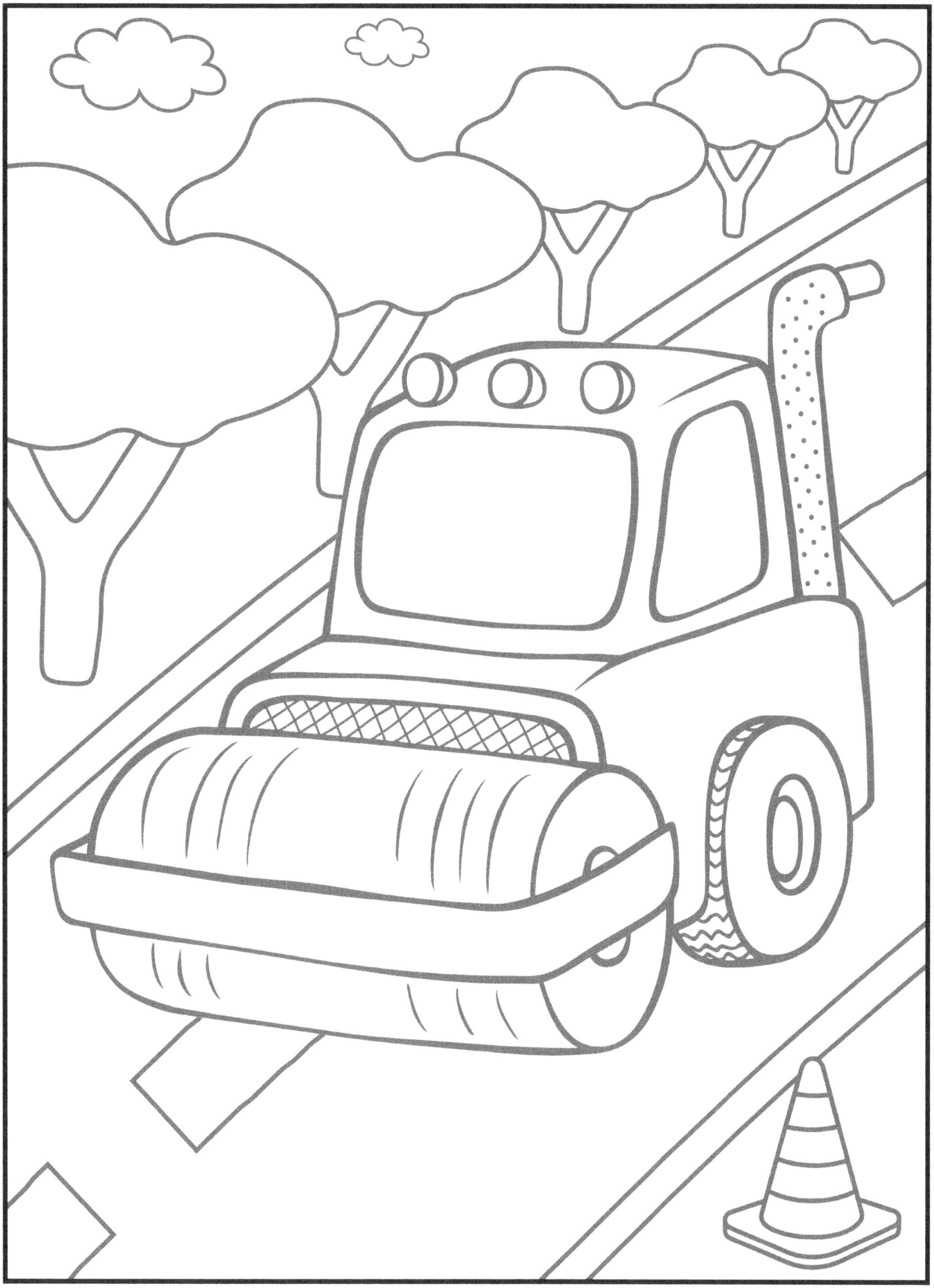

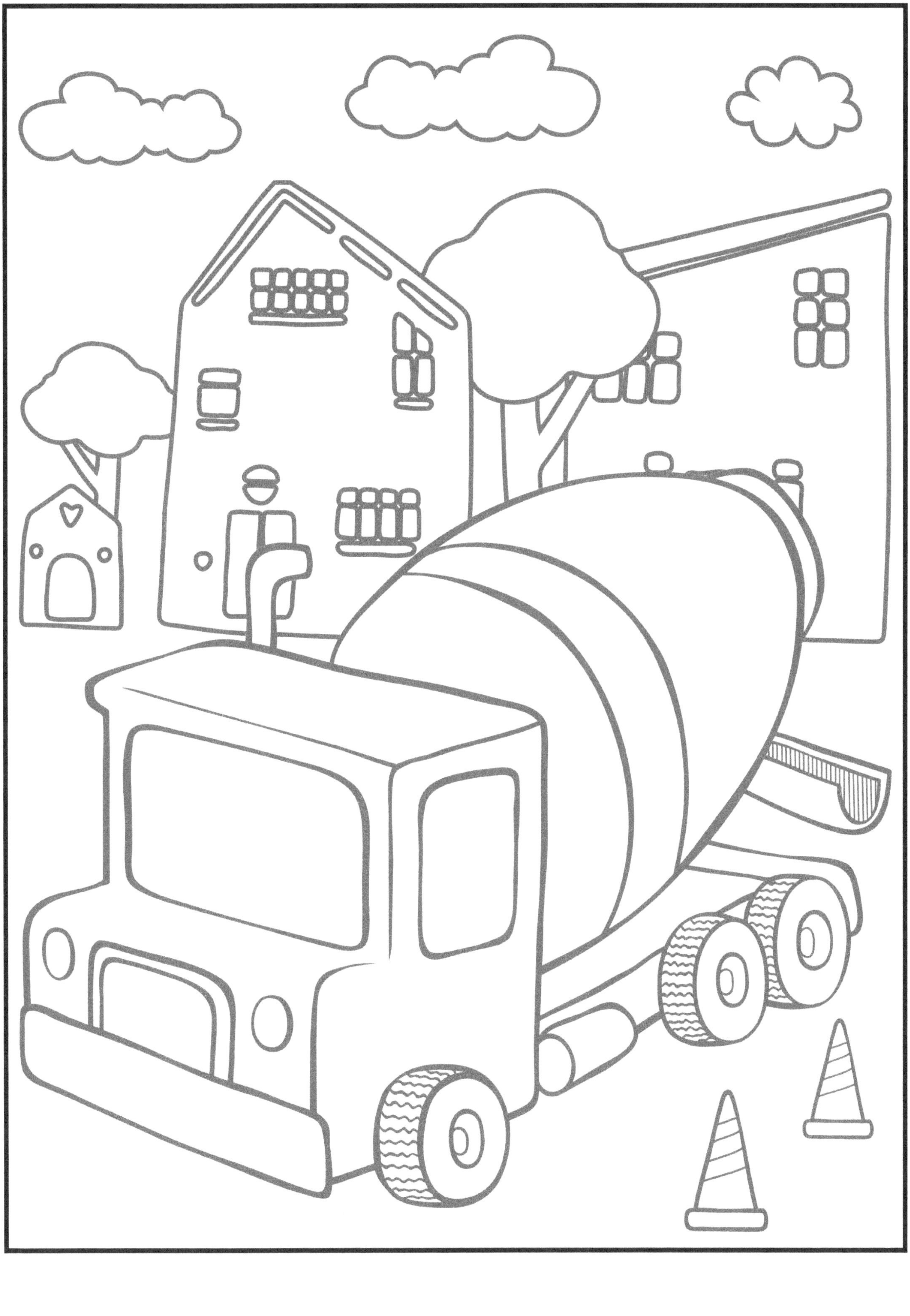

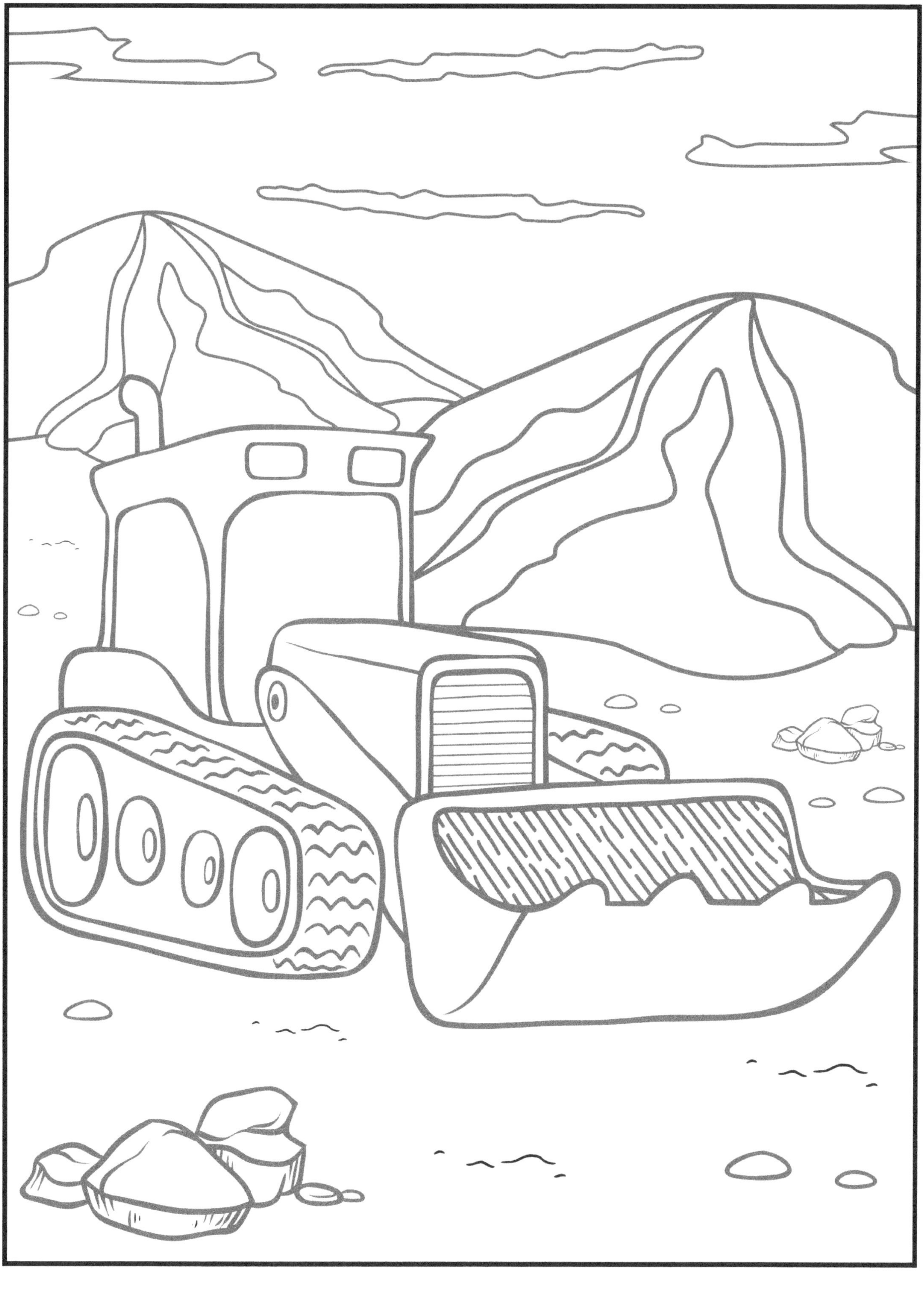

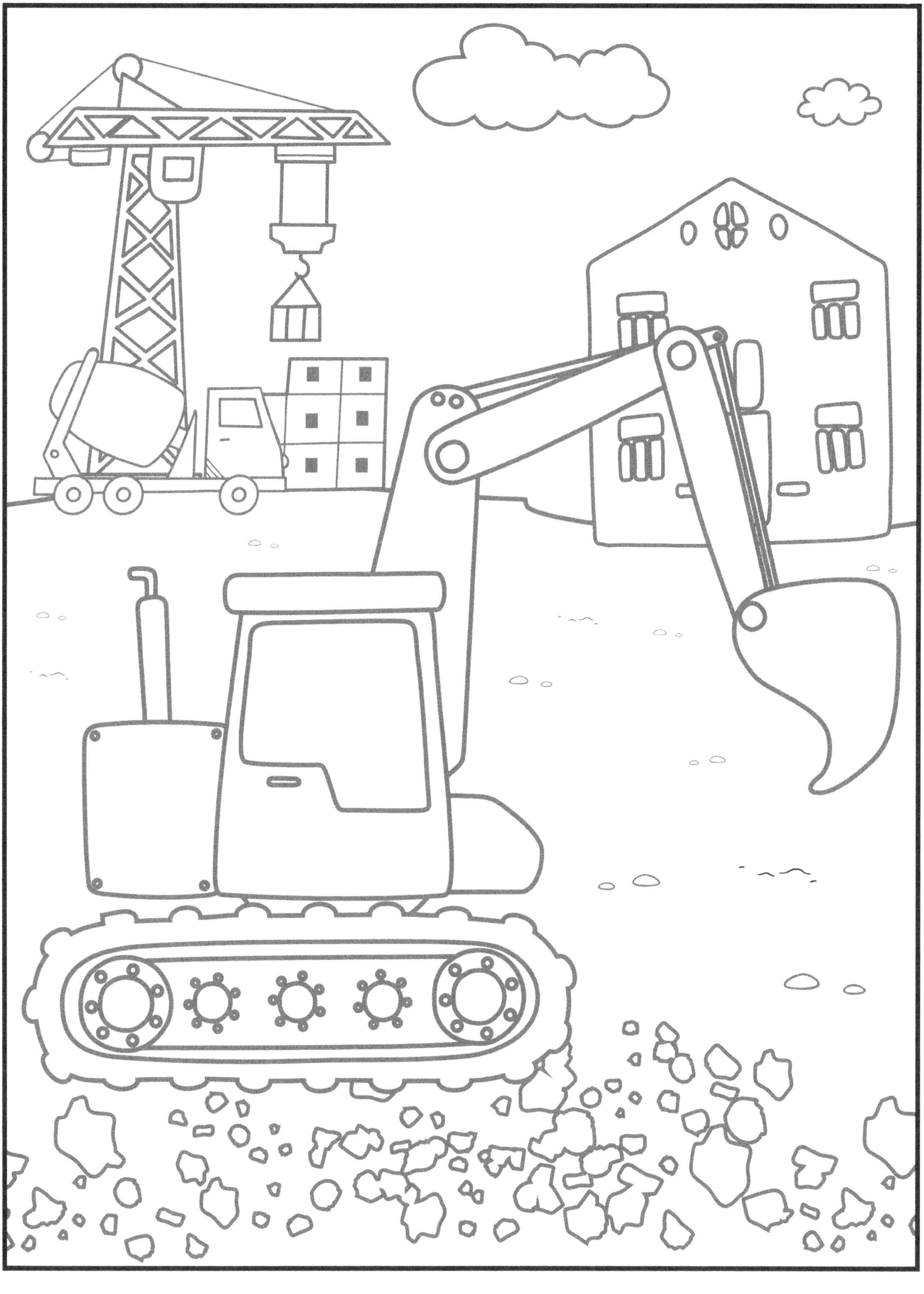

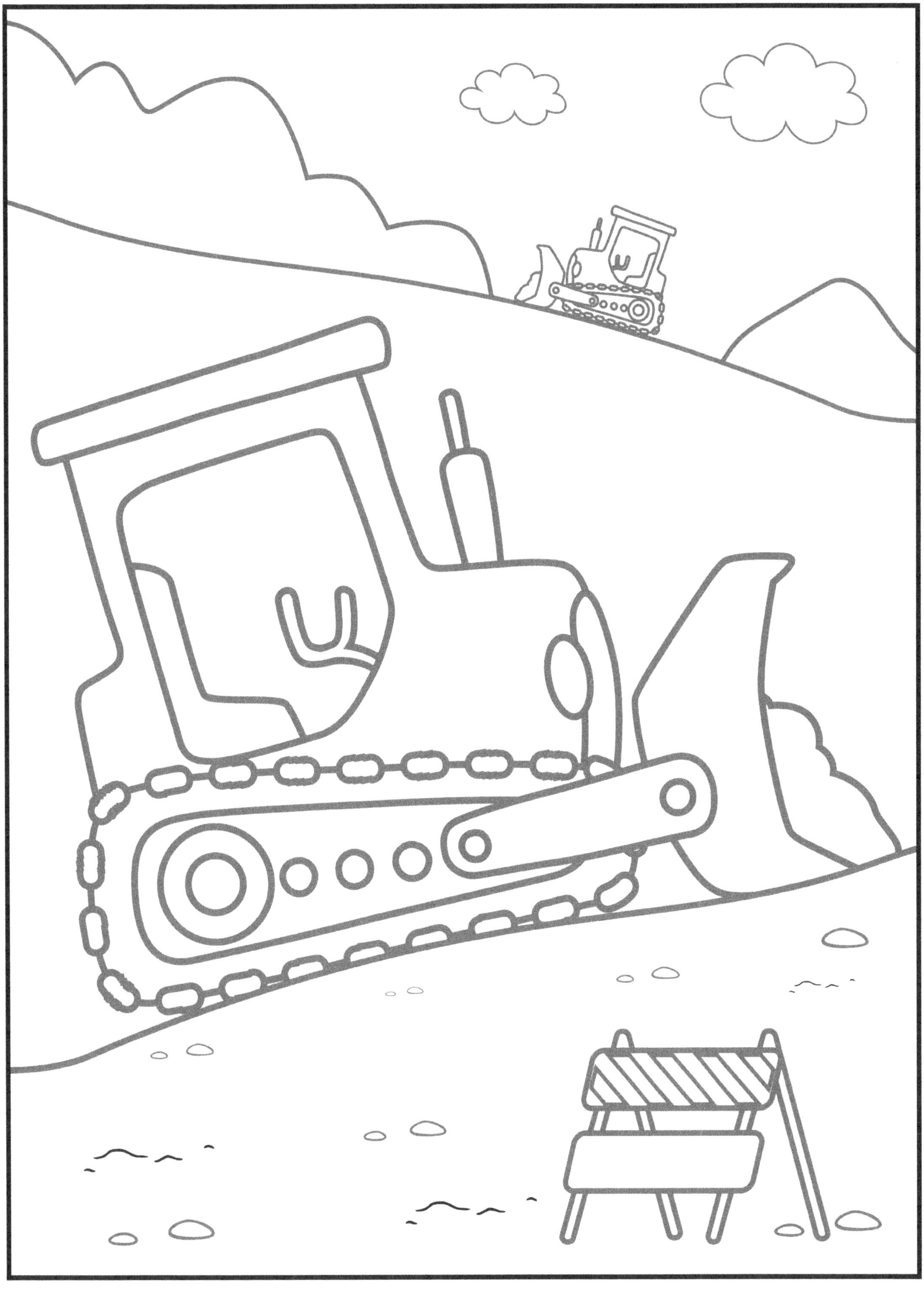

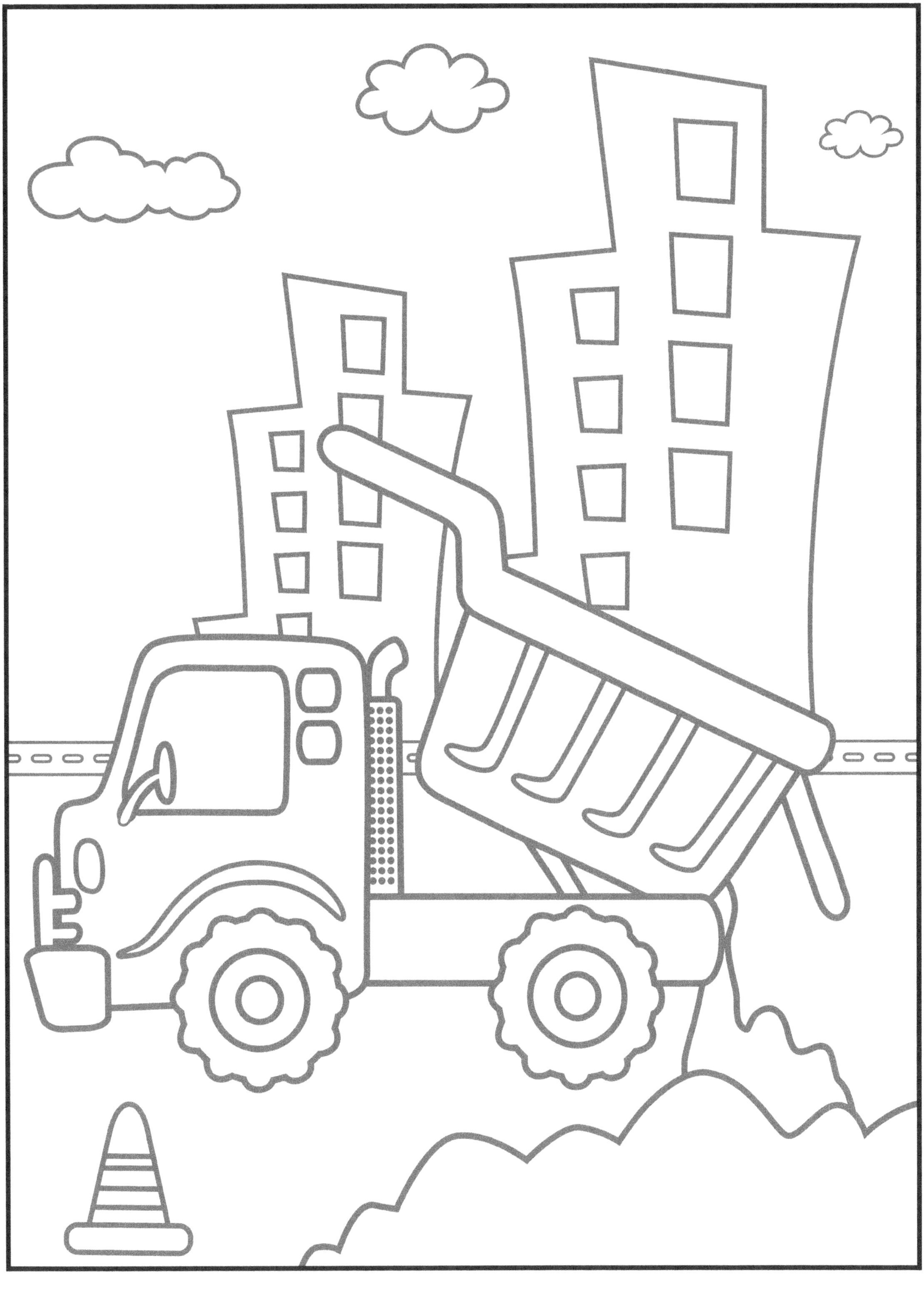

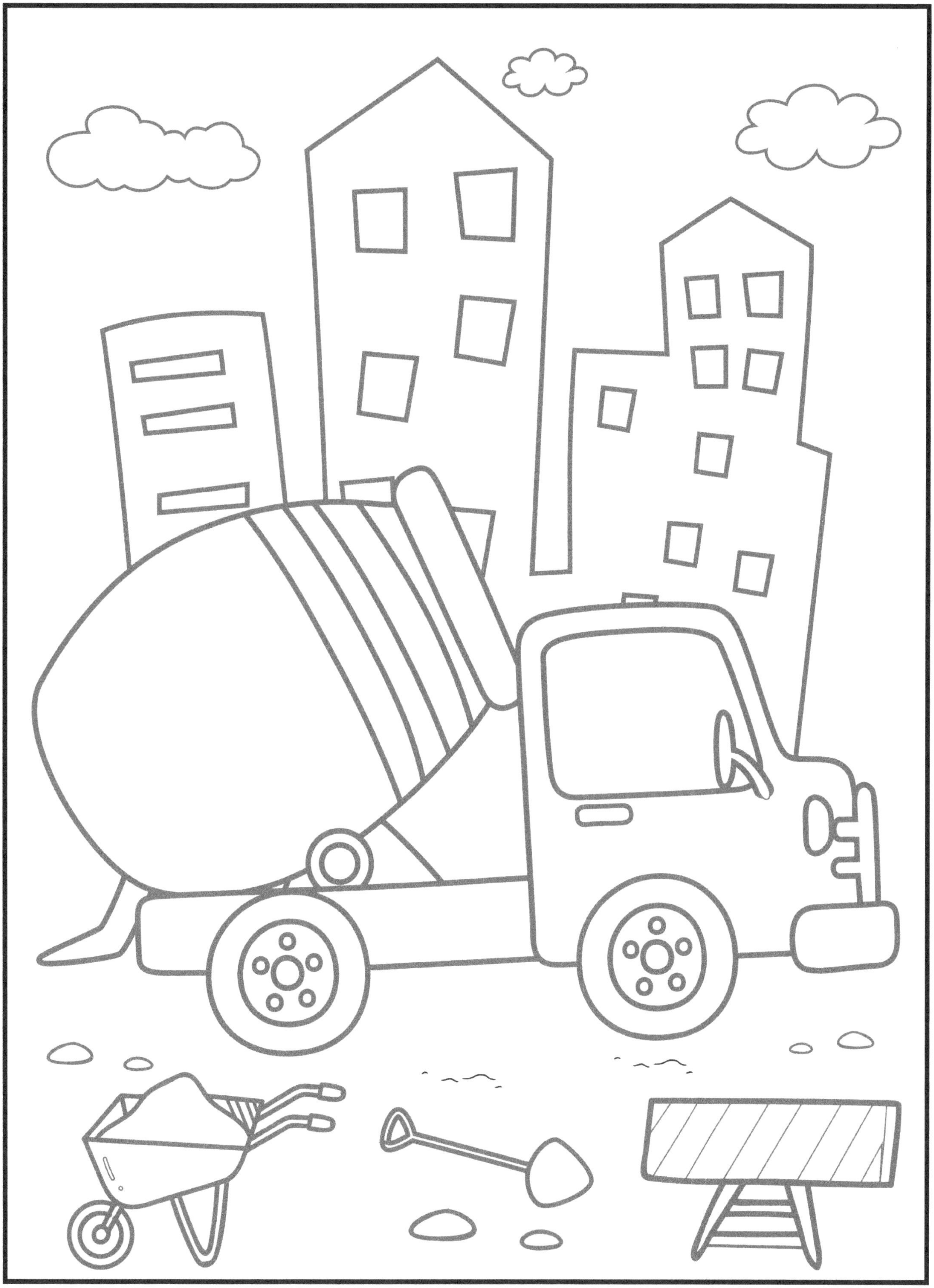

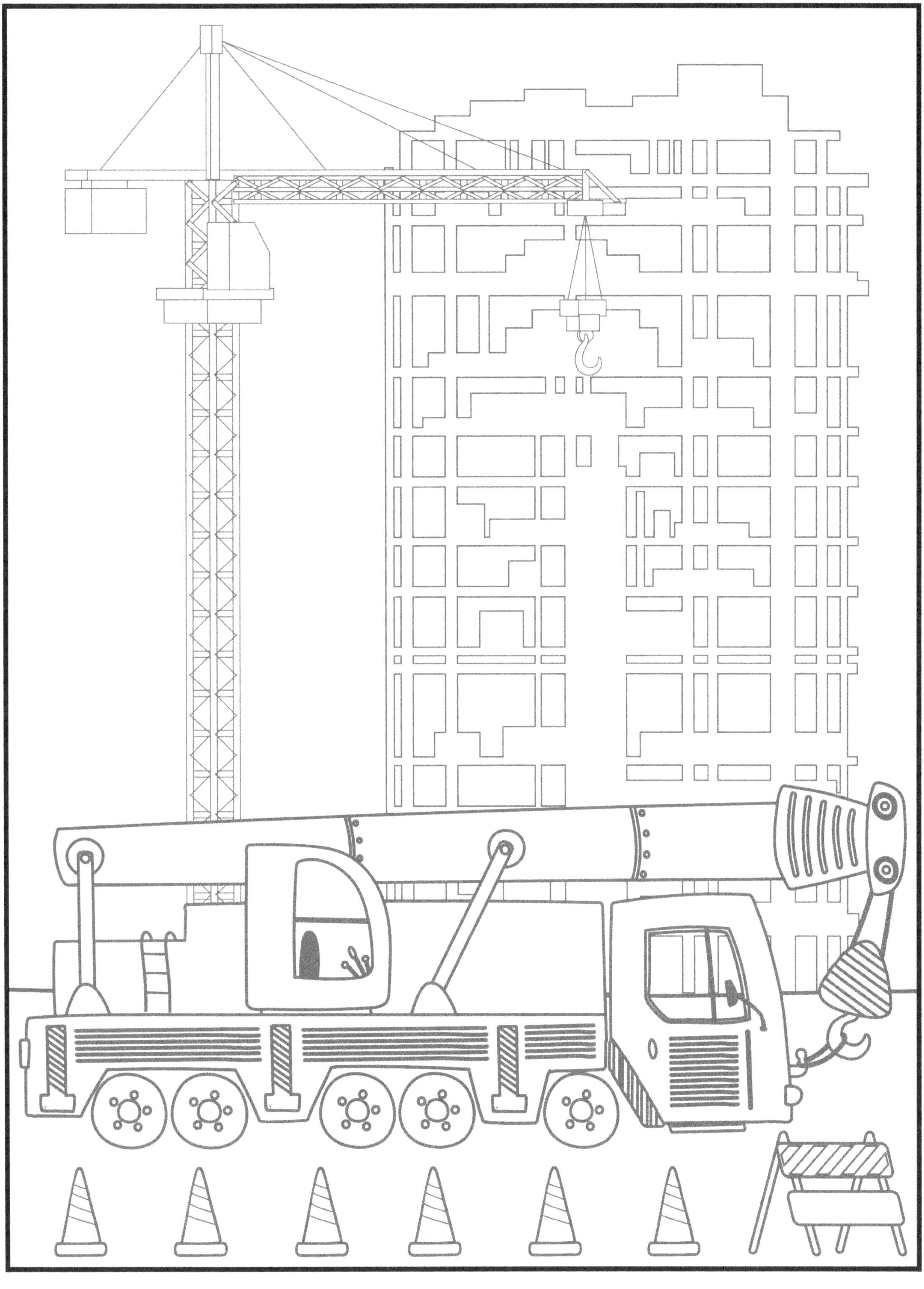

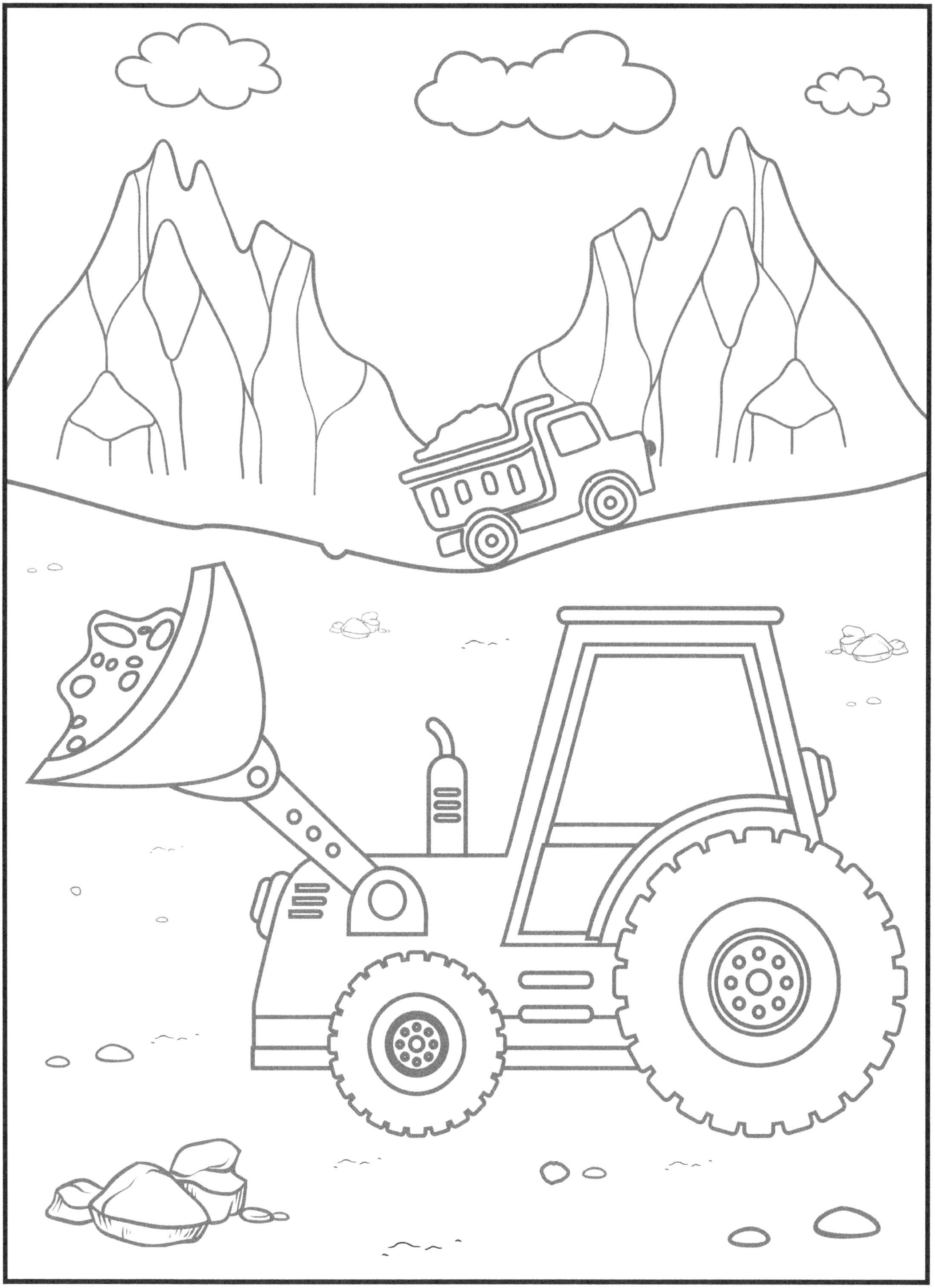

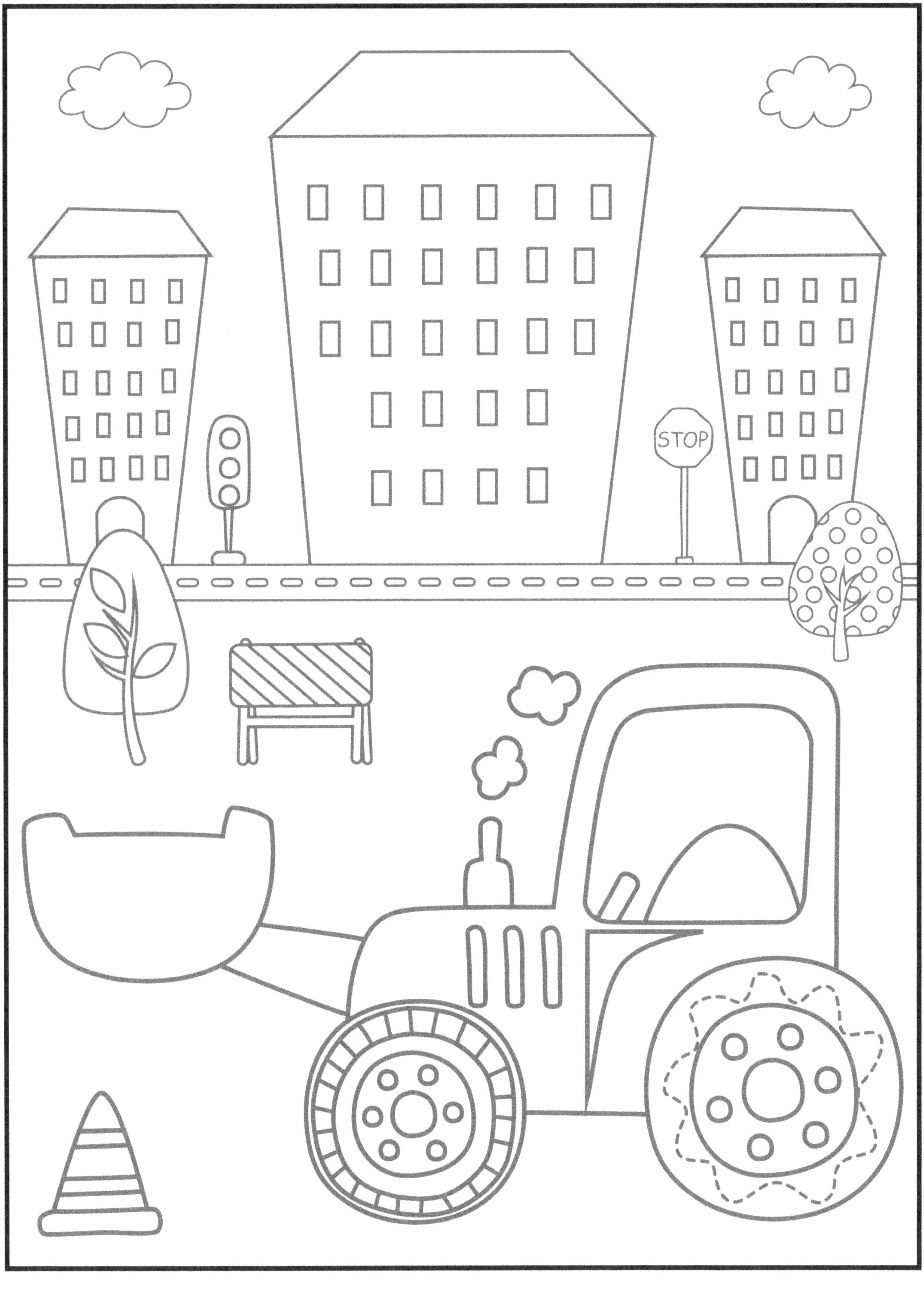
STOP

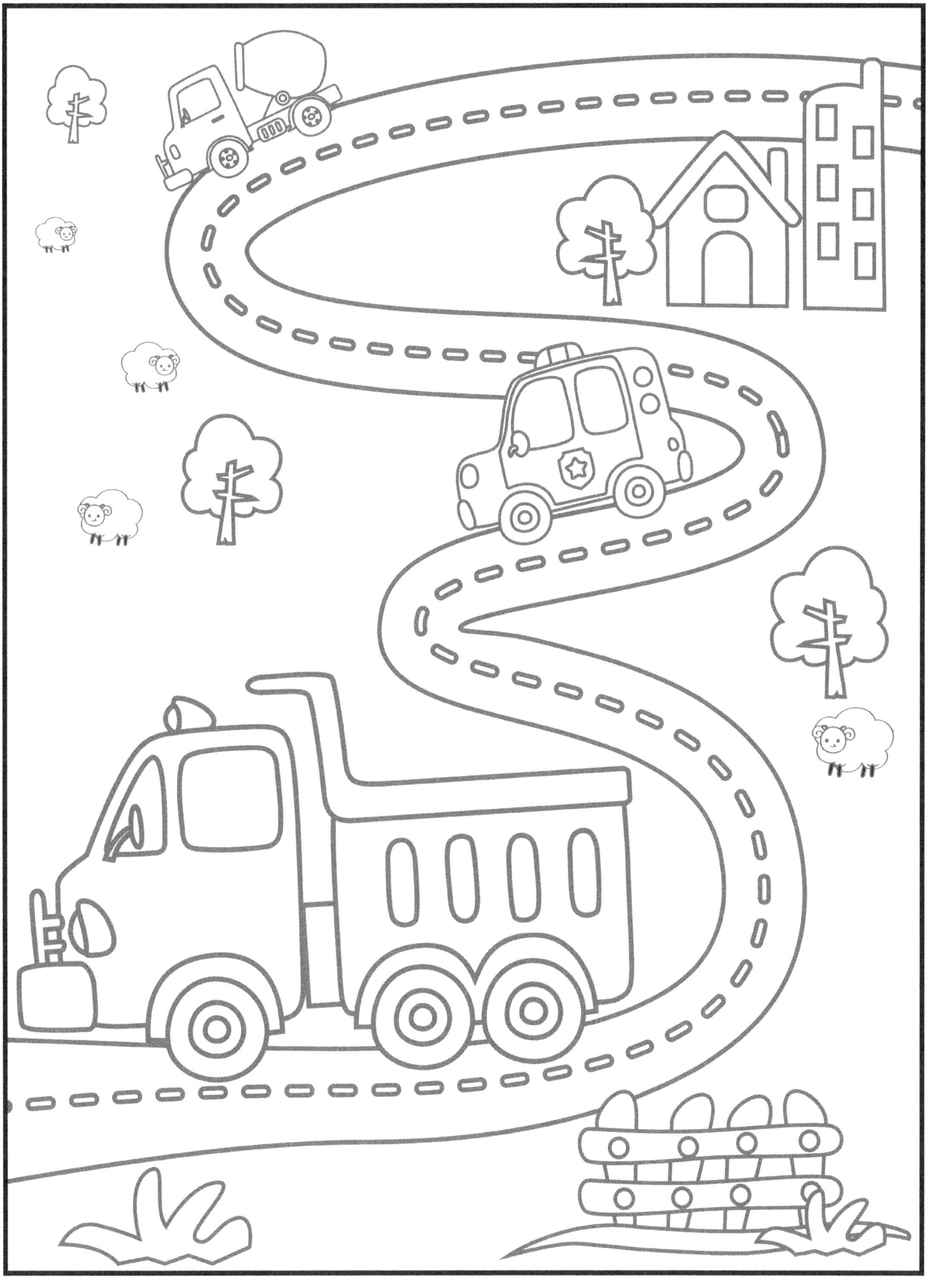

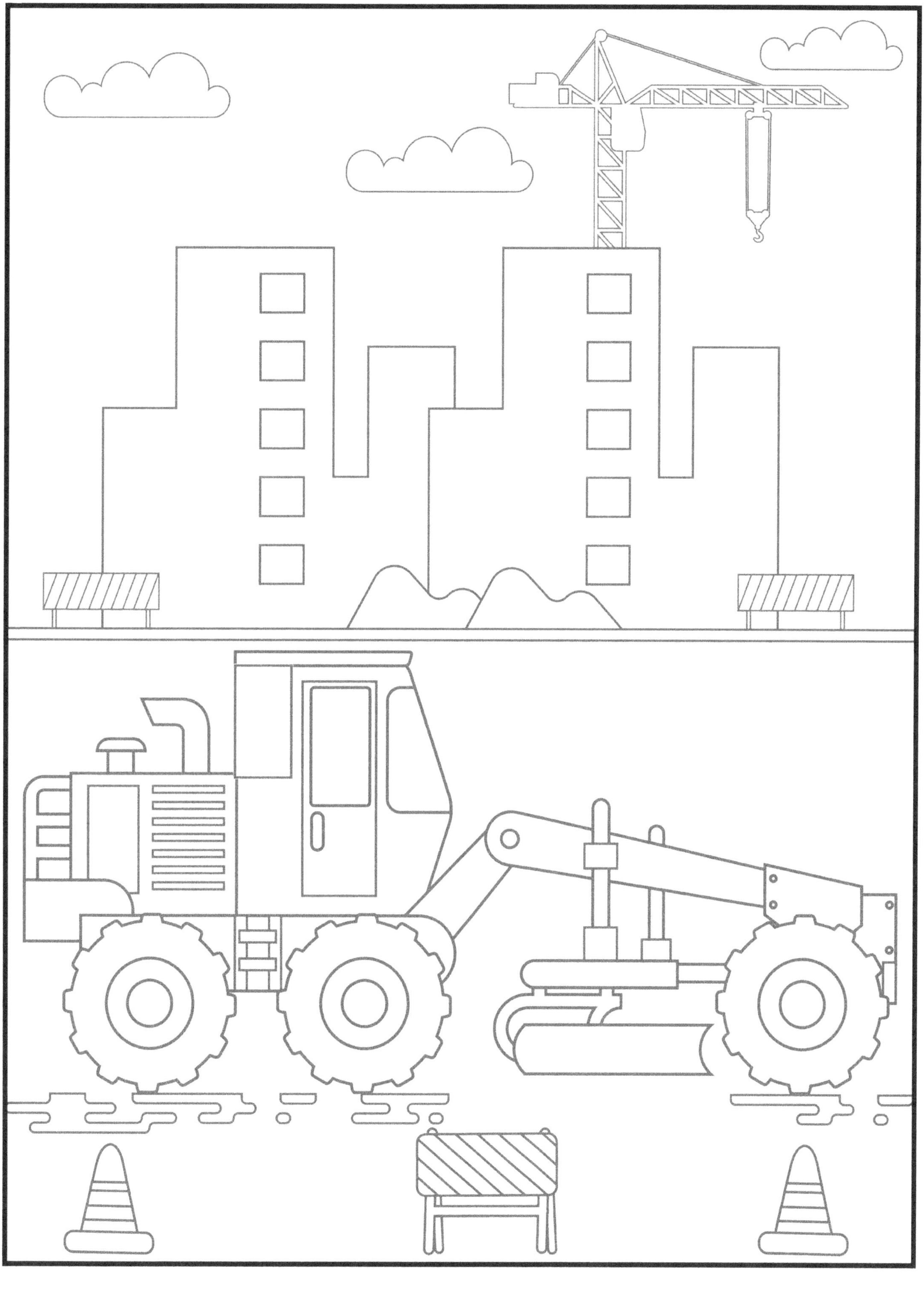

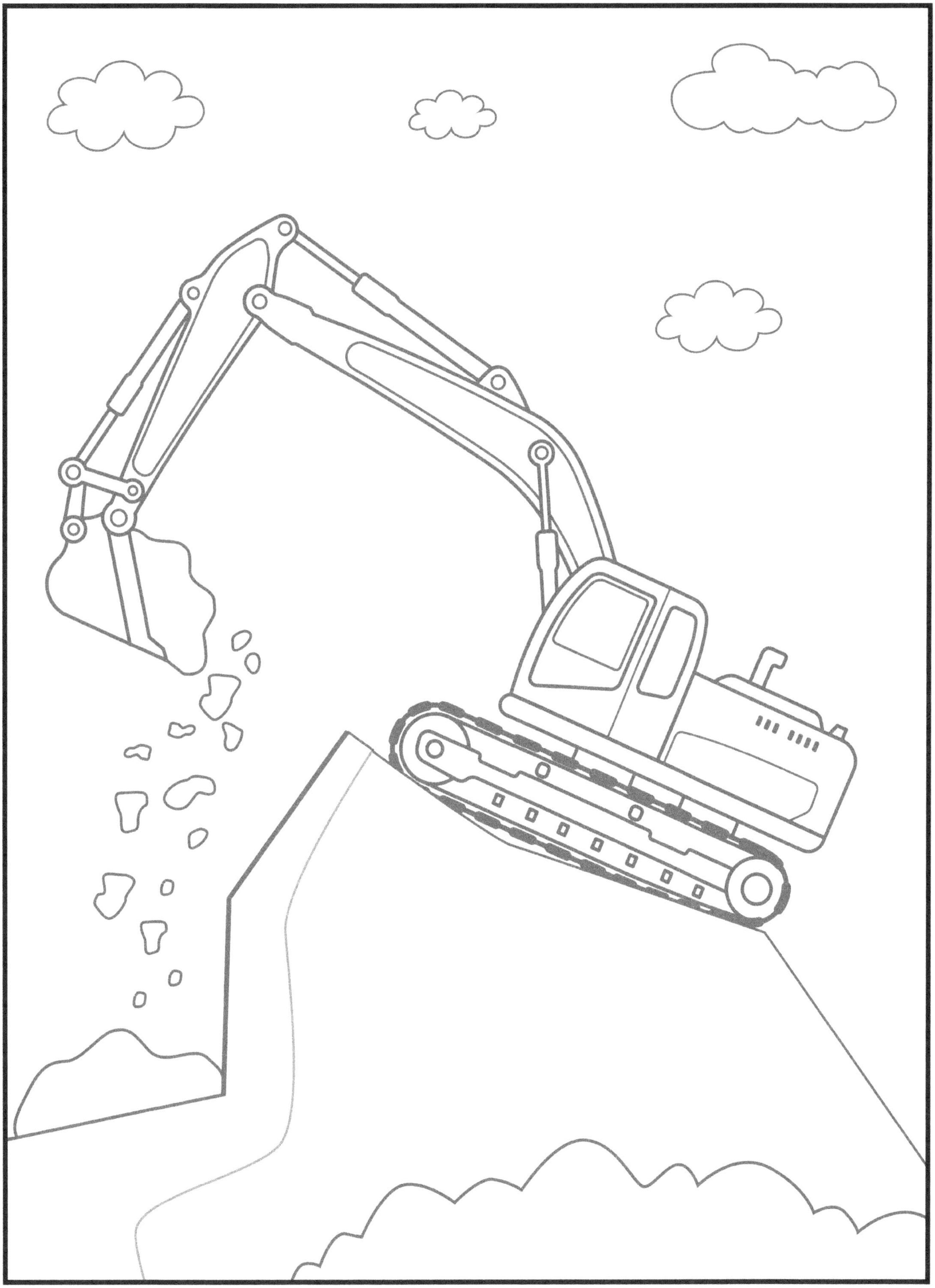

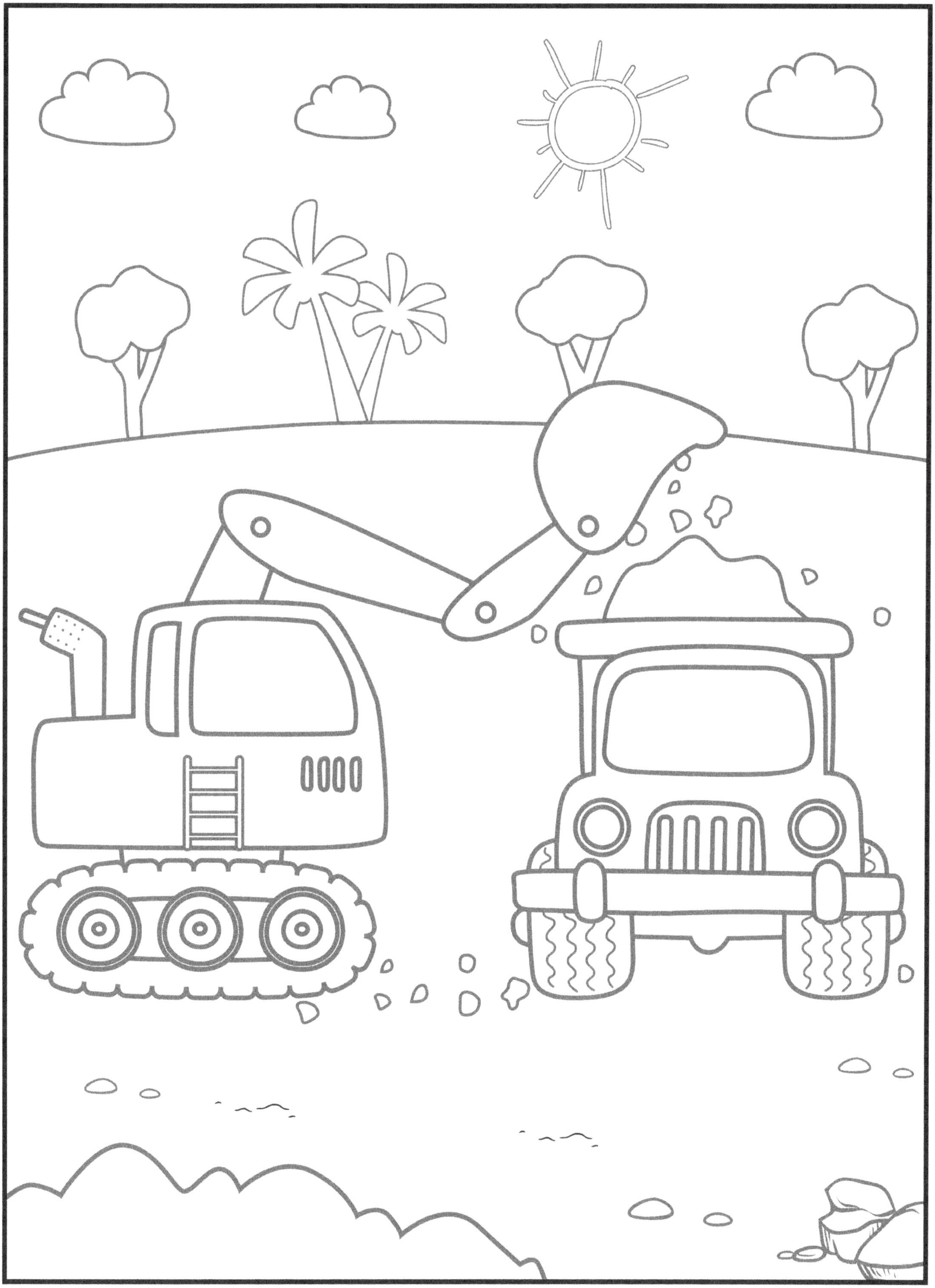

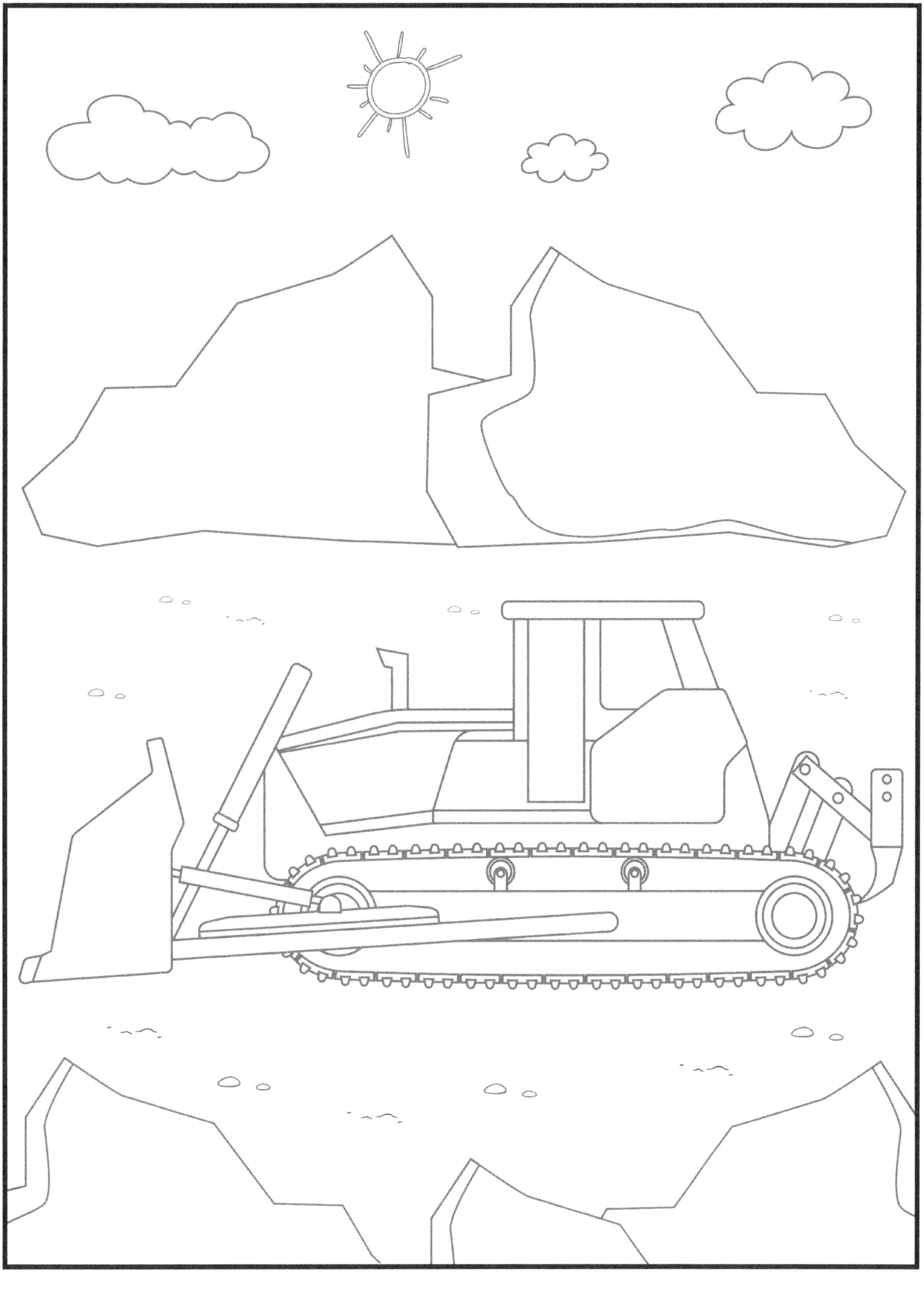

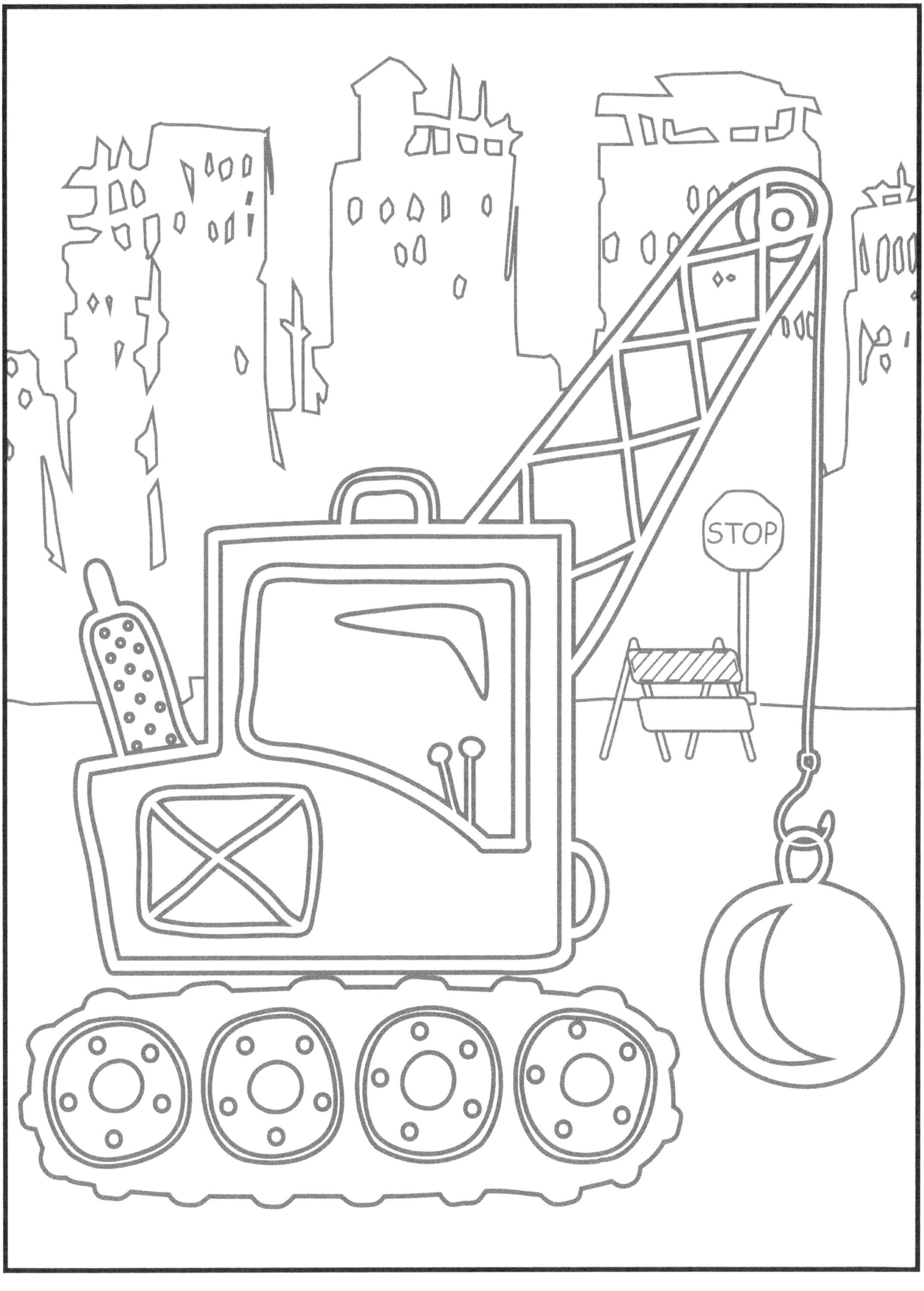
STOP

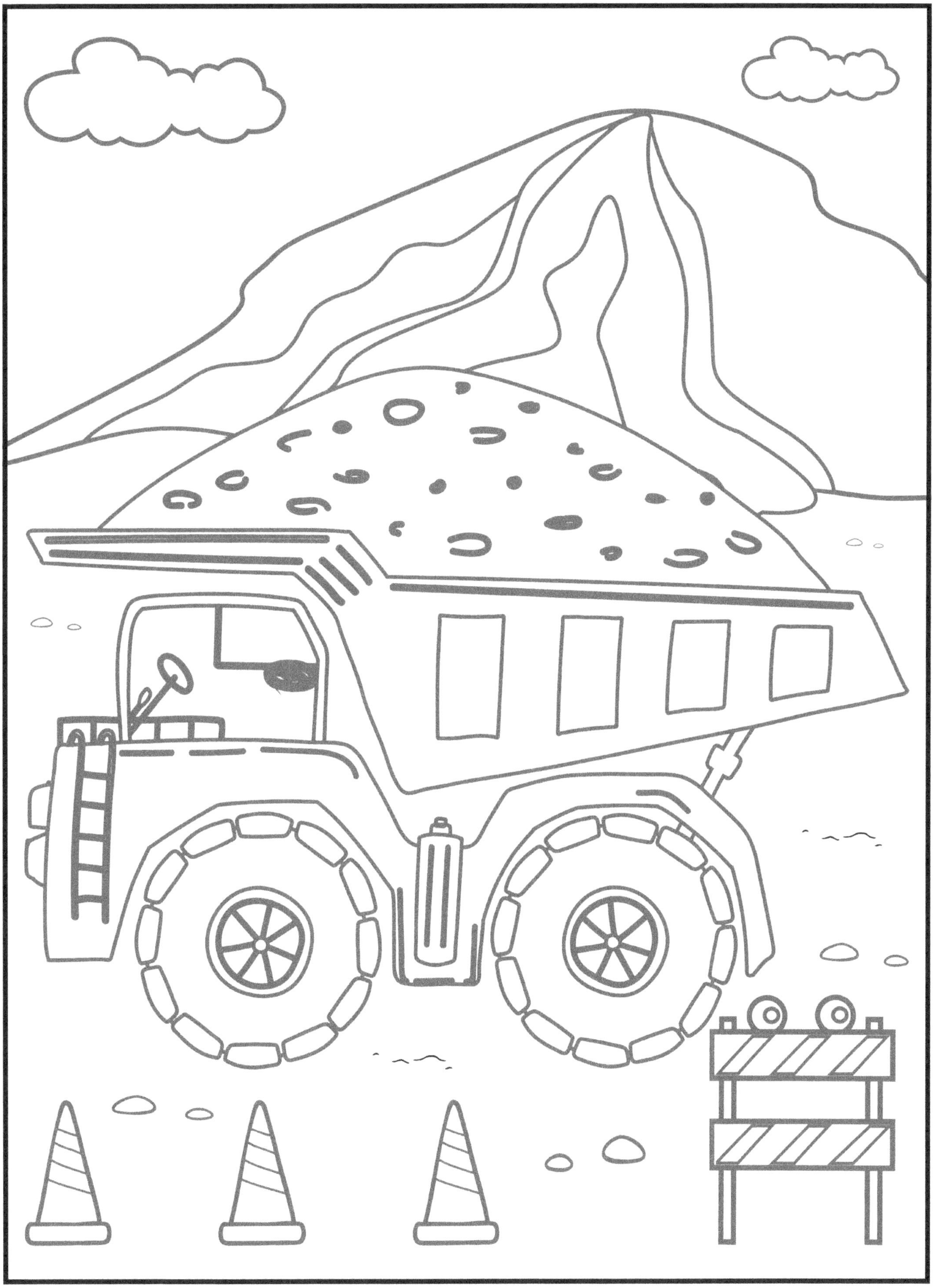

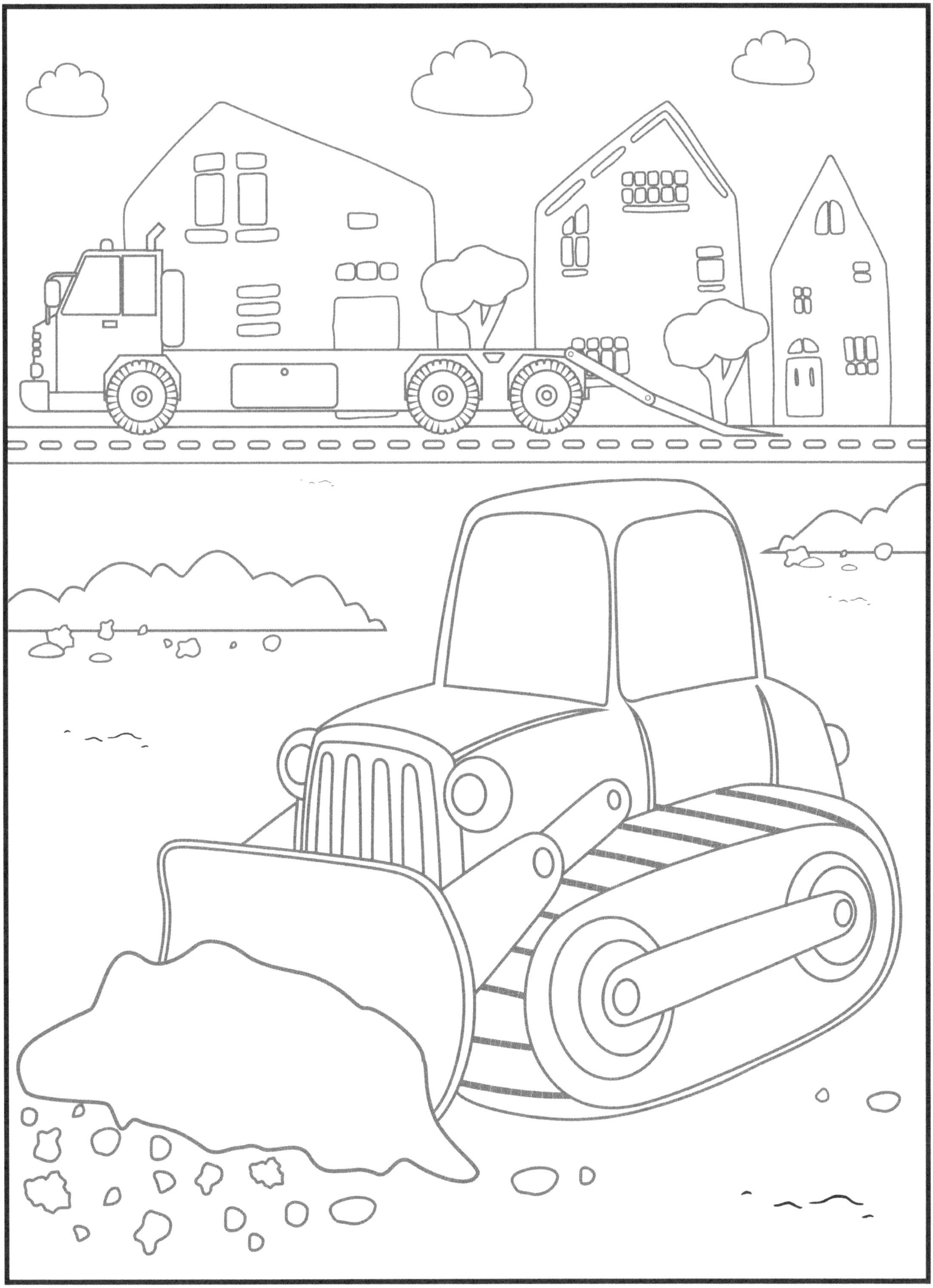

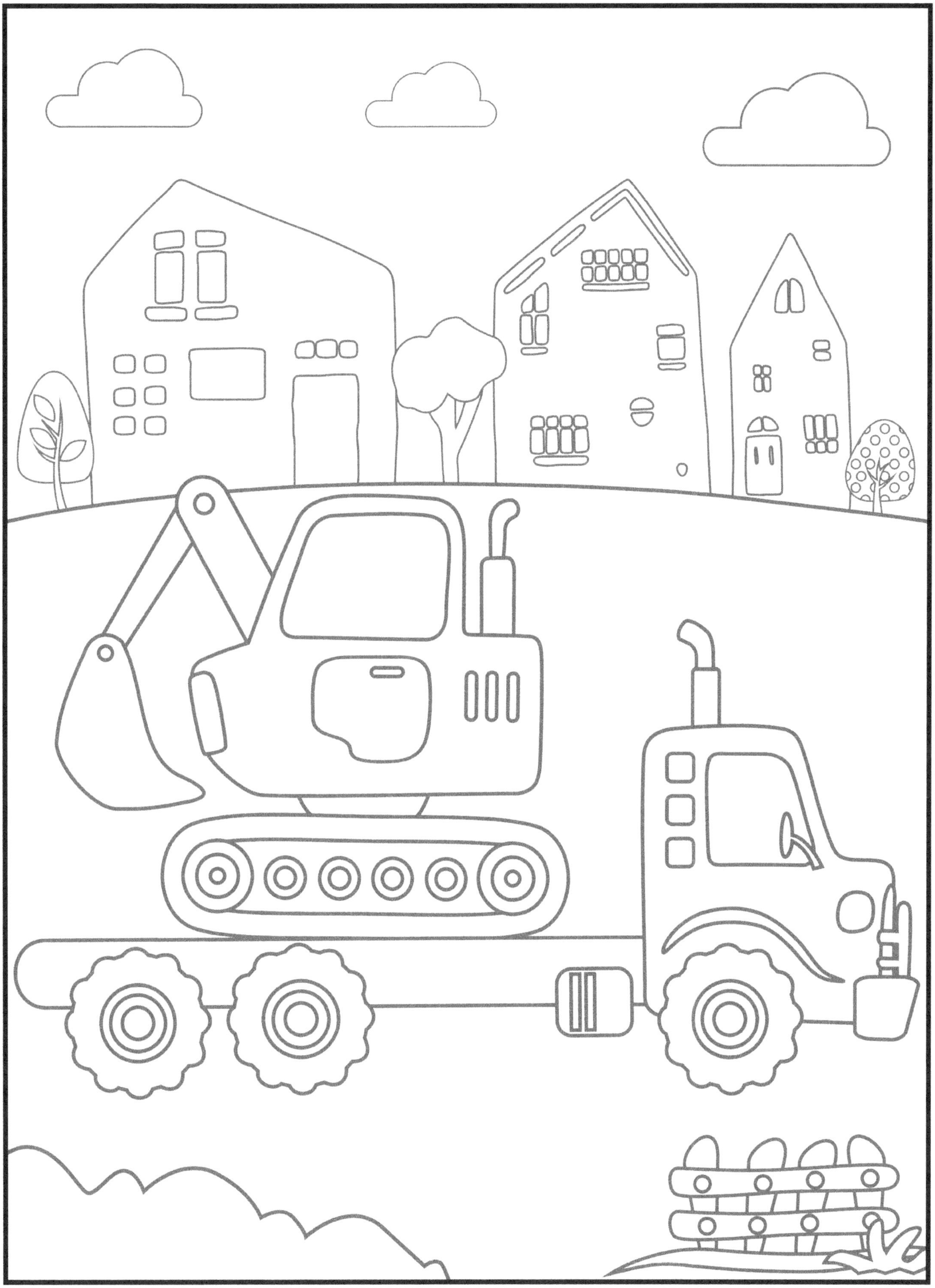

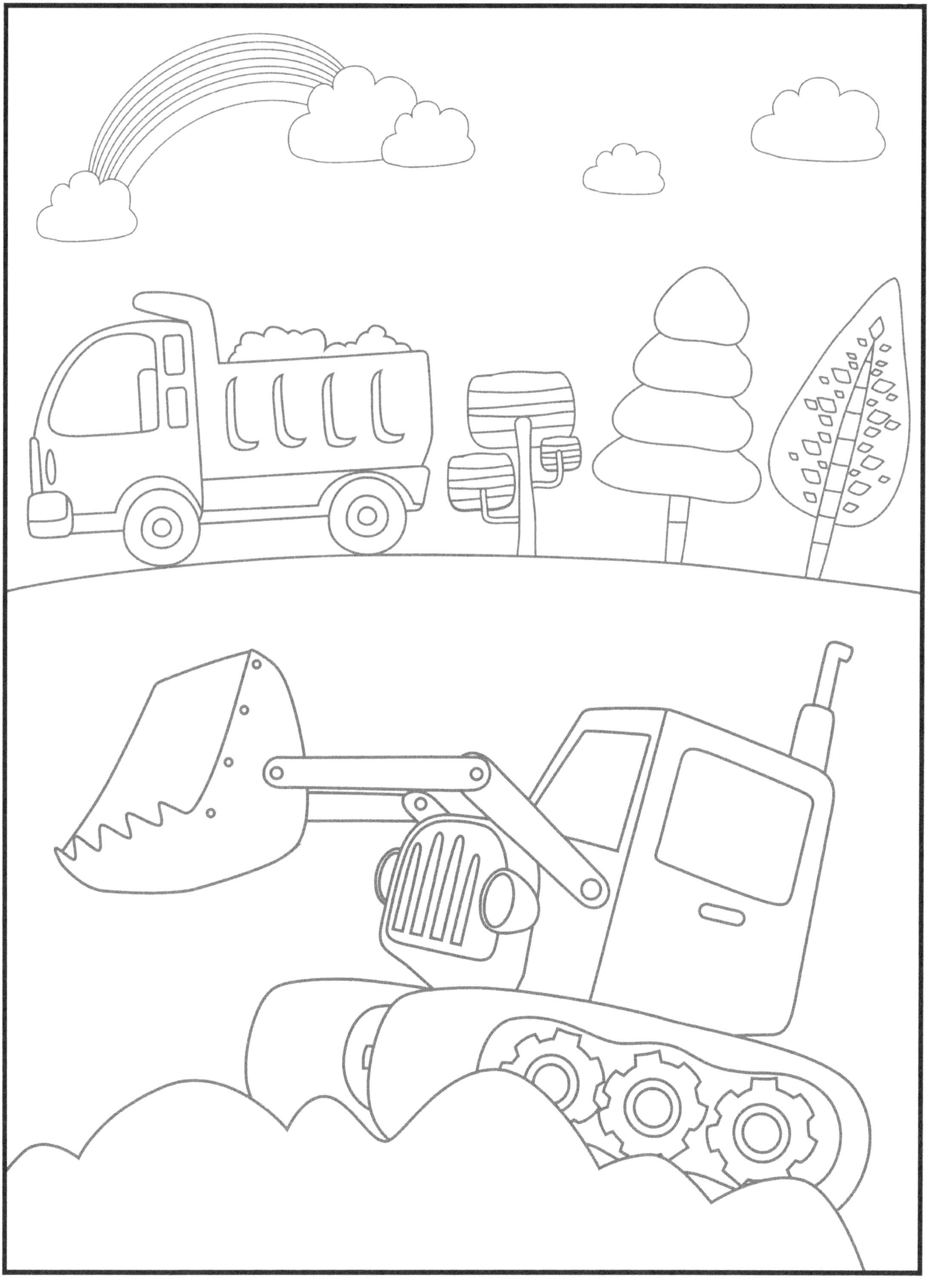

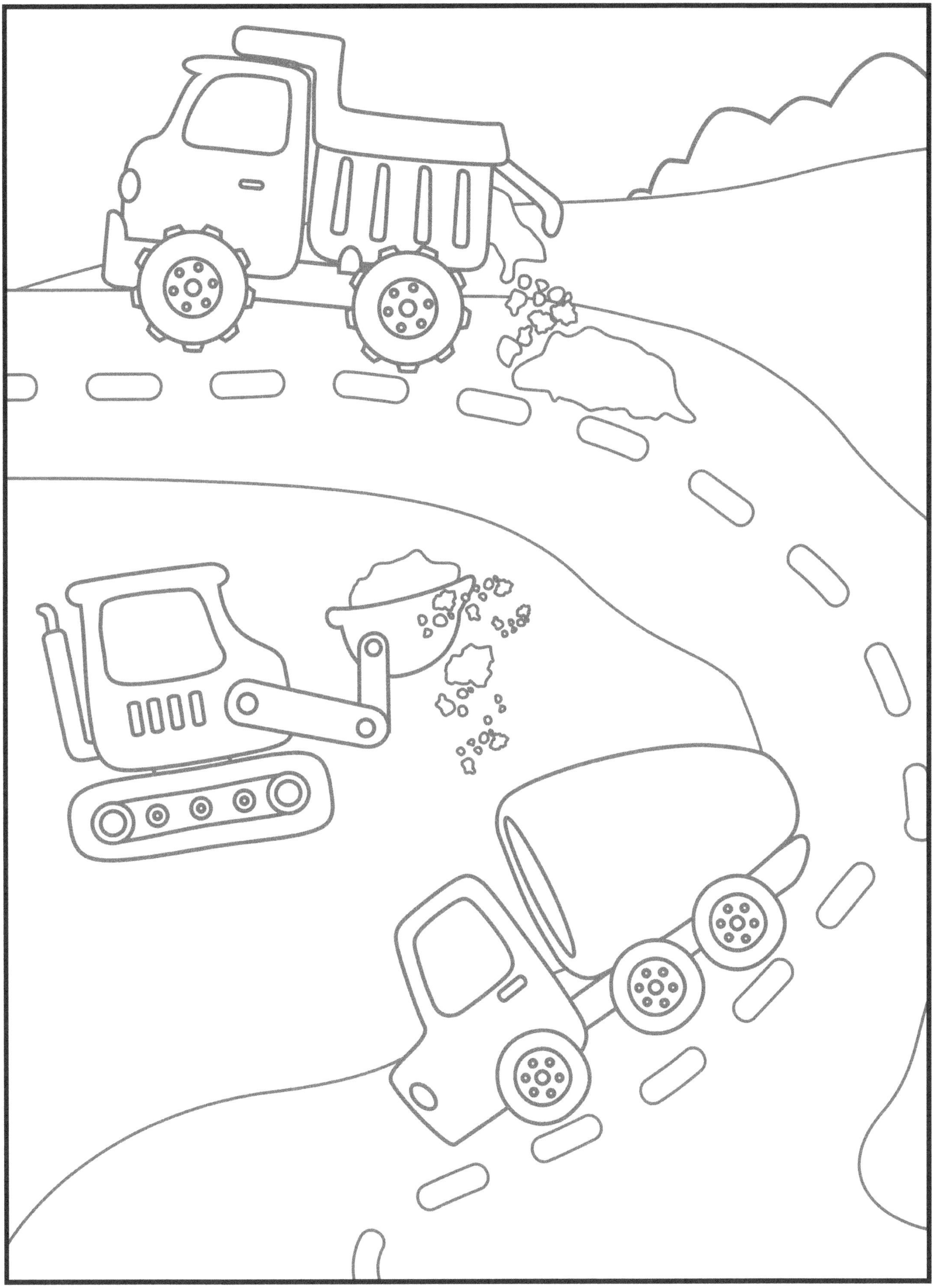

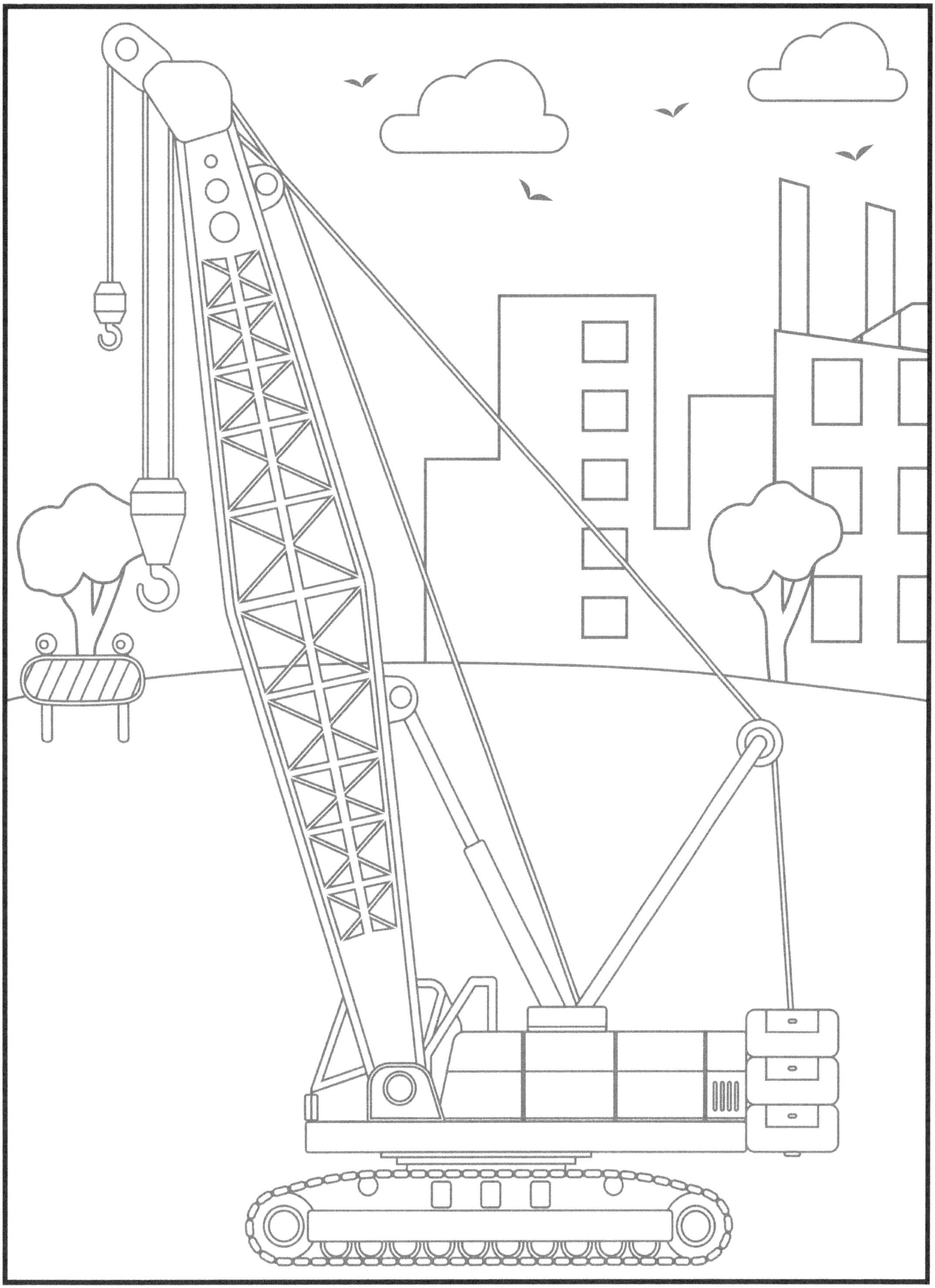

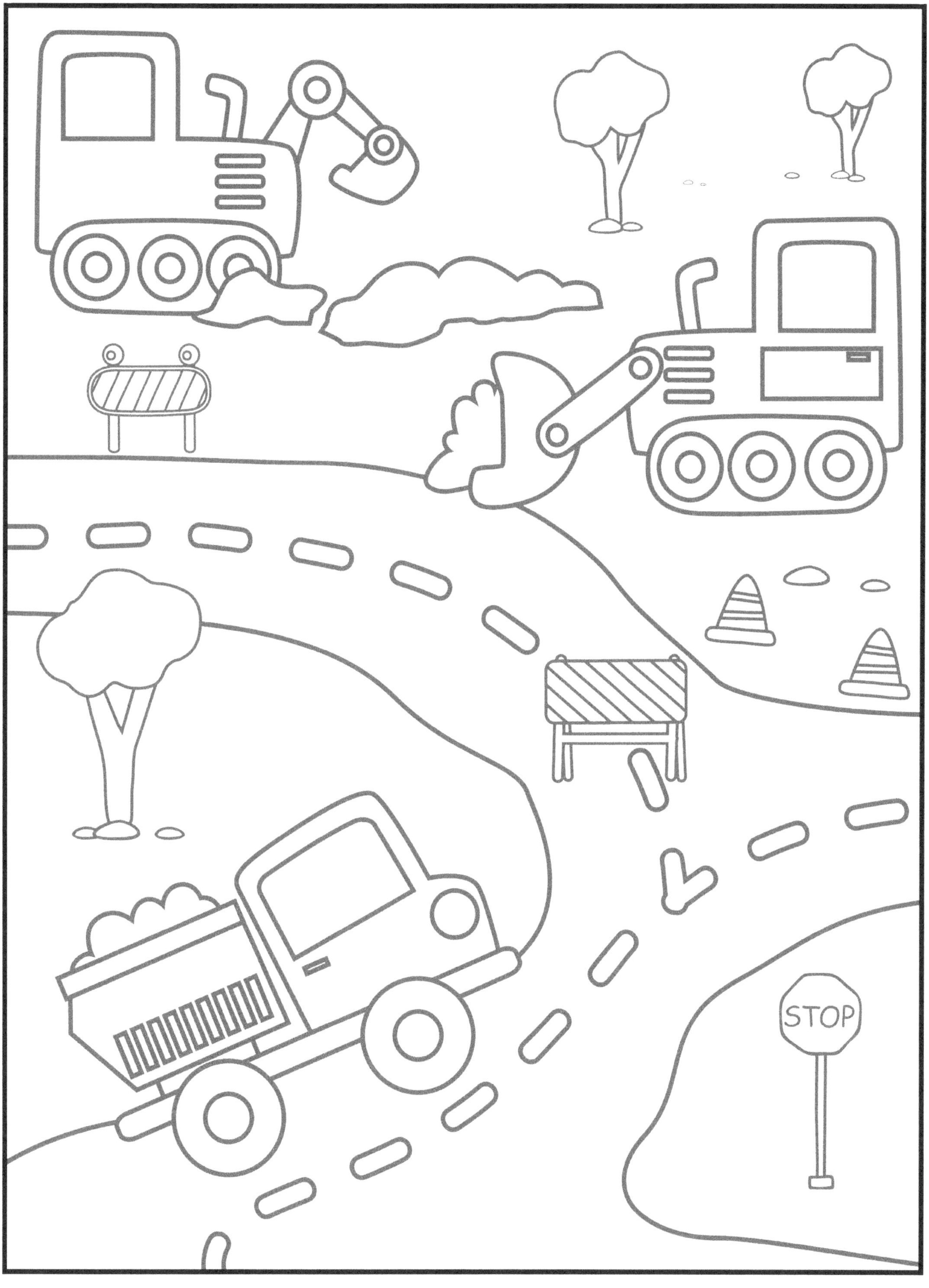
STOP

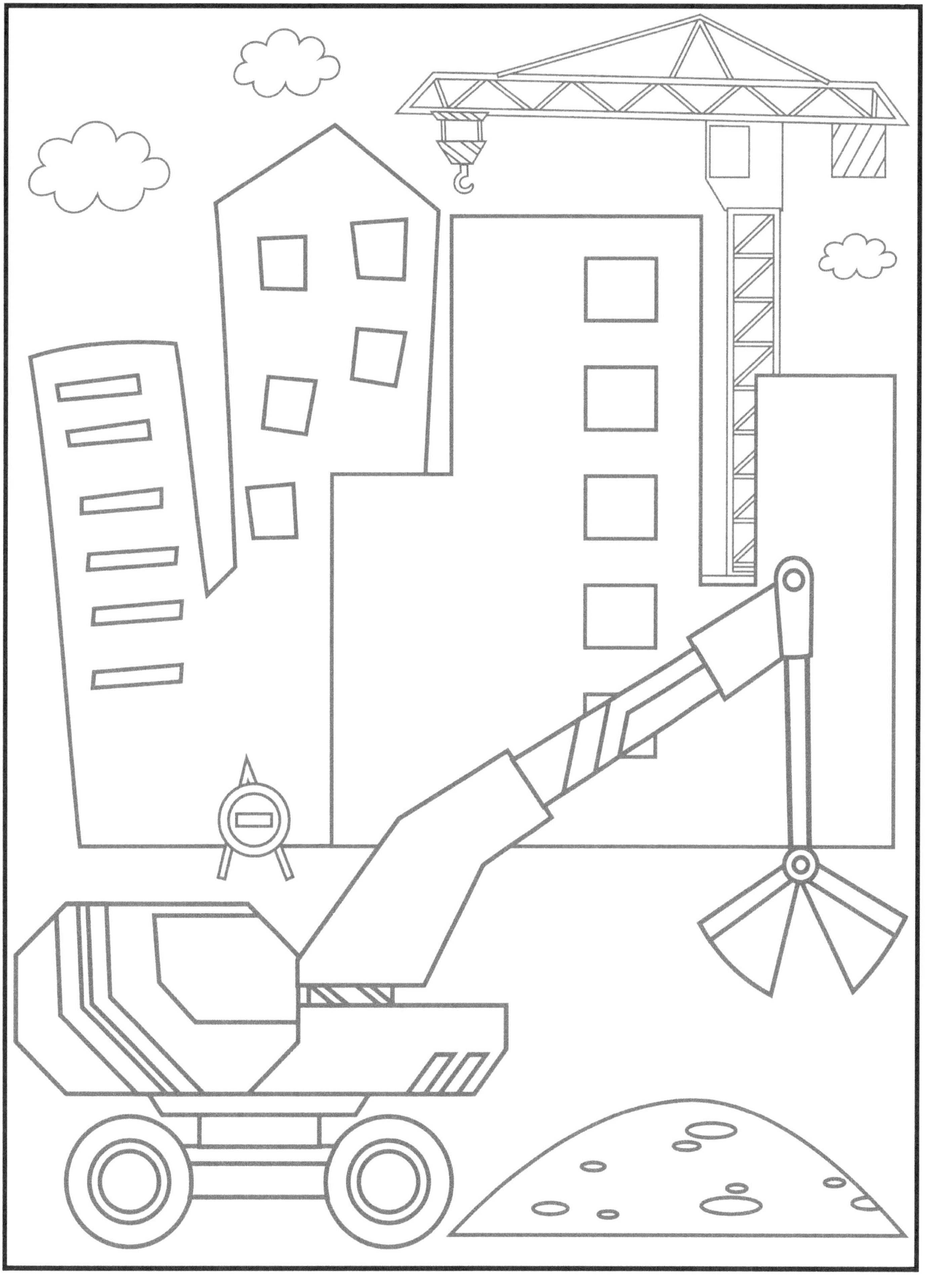

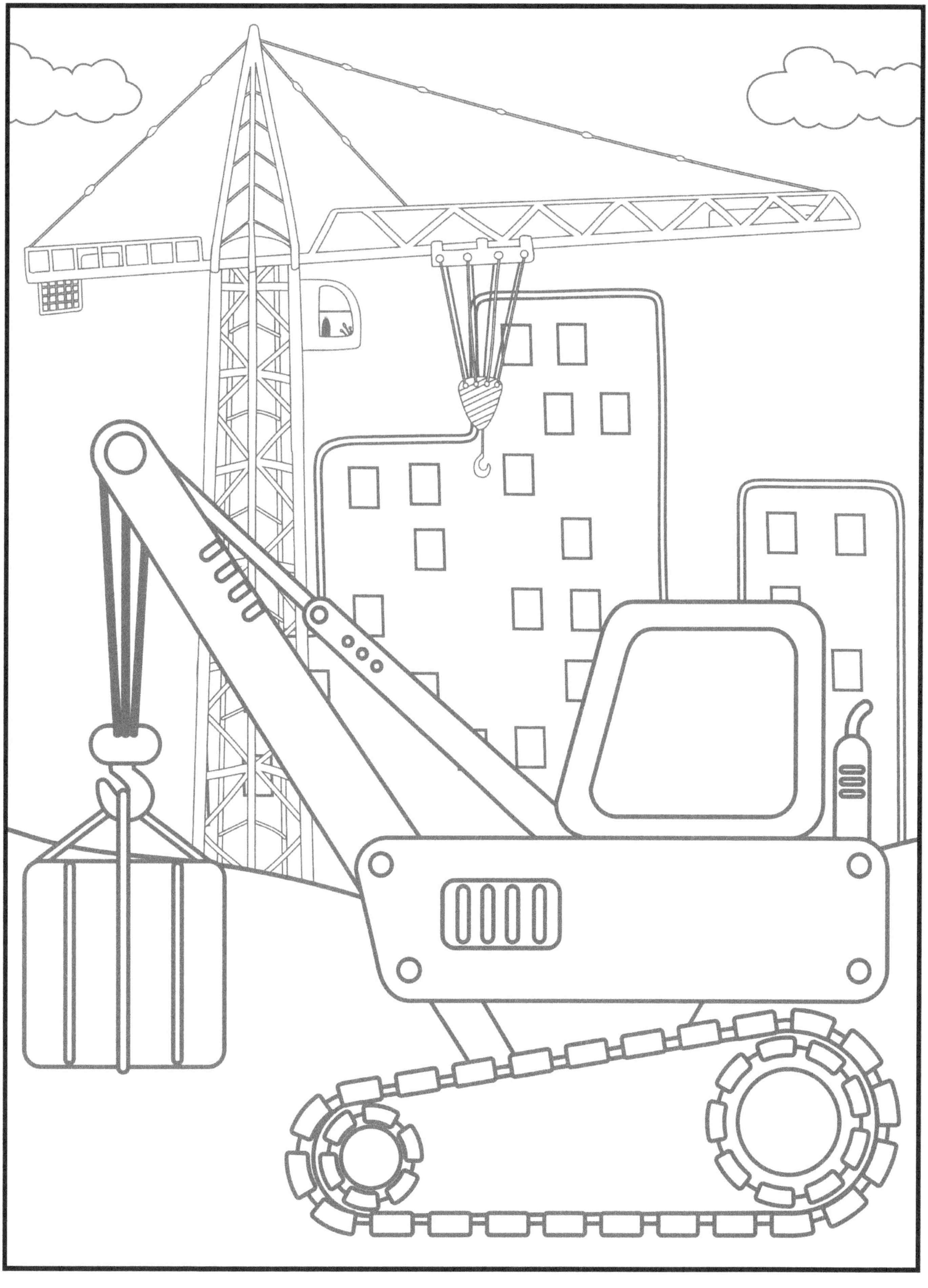

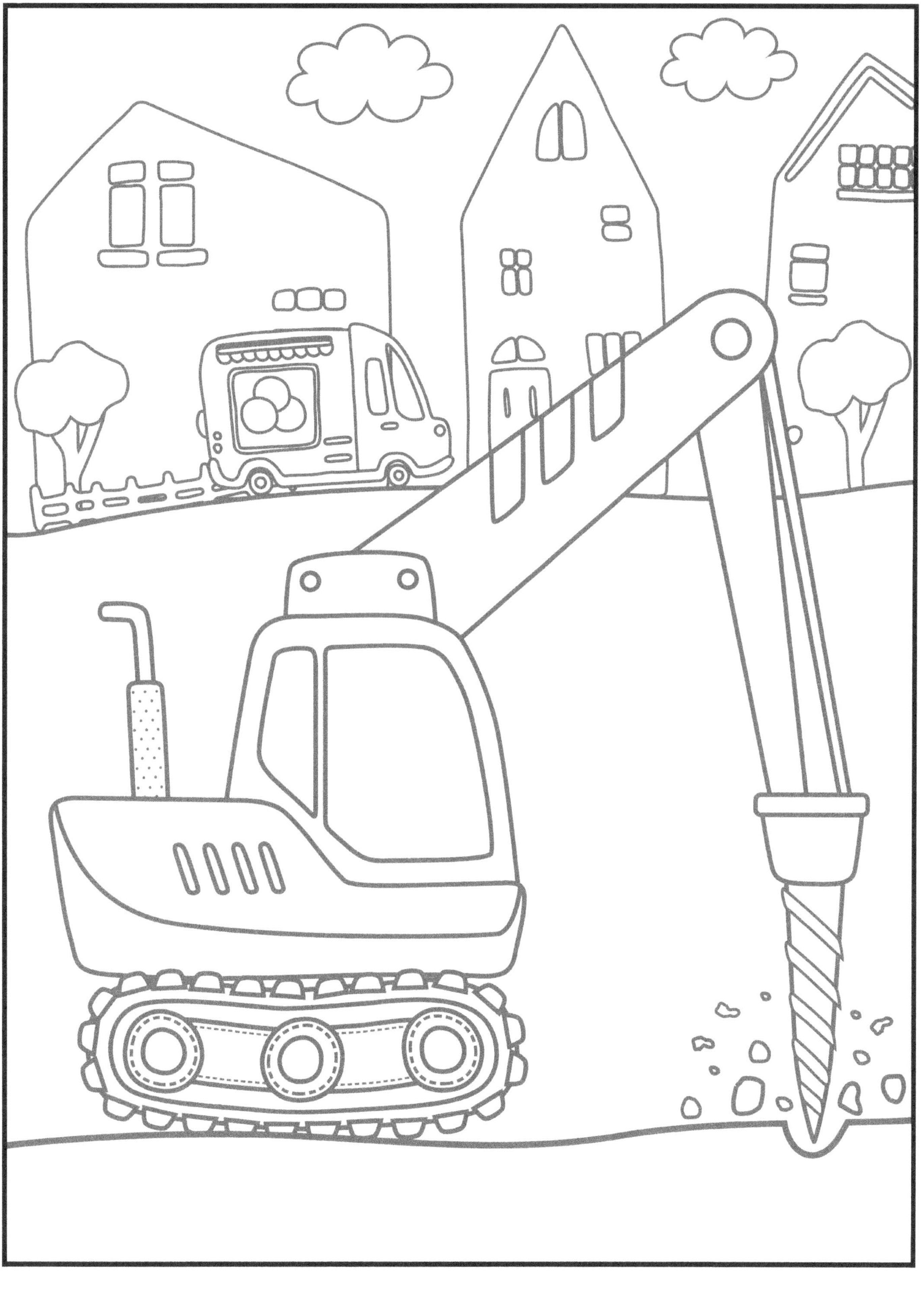

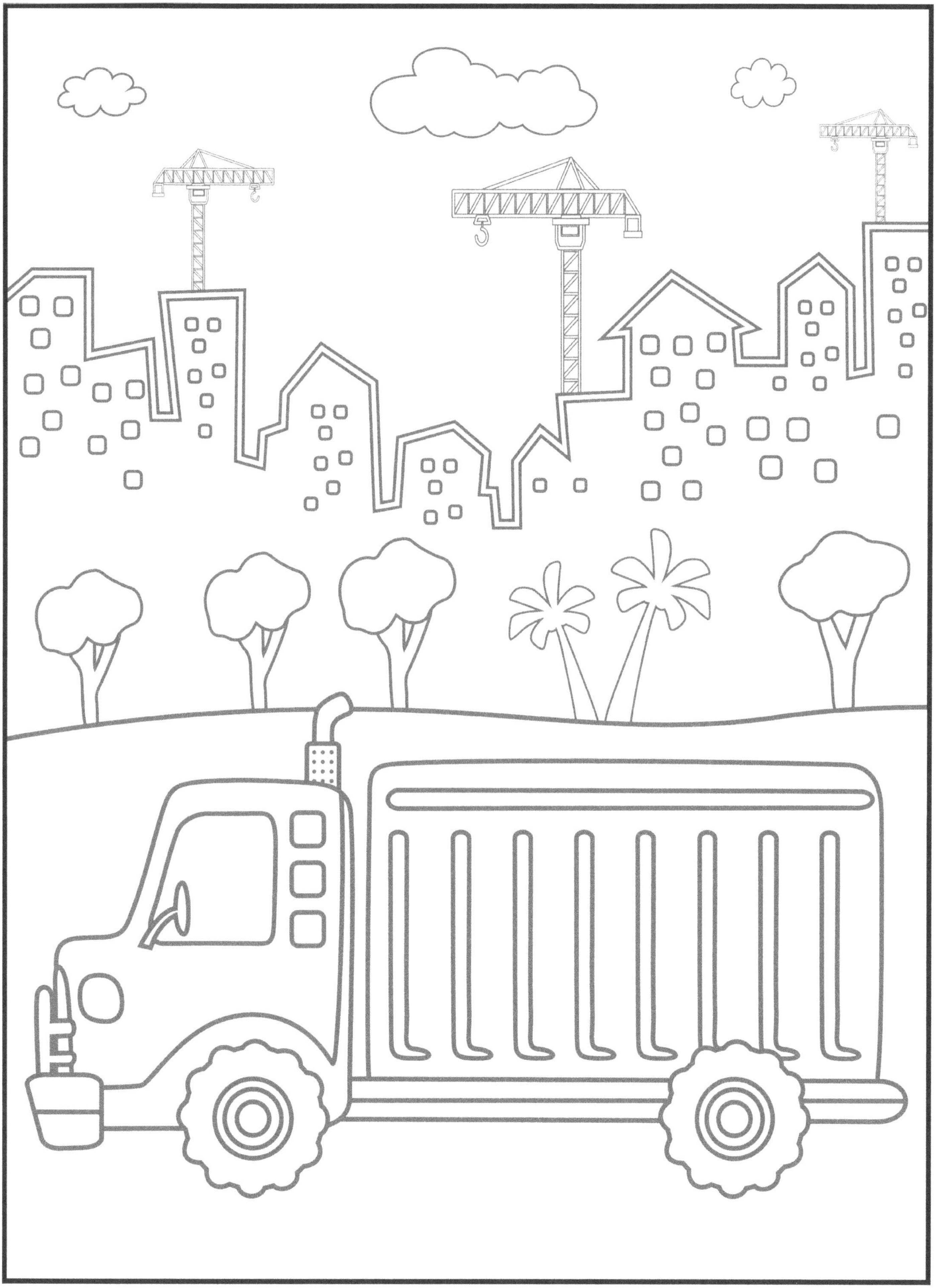

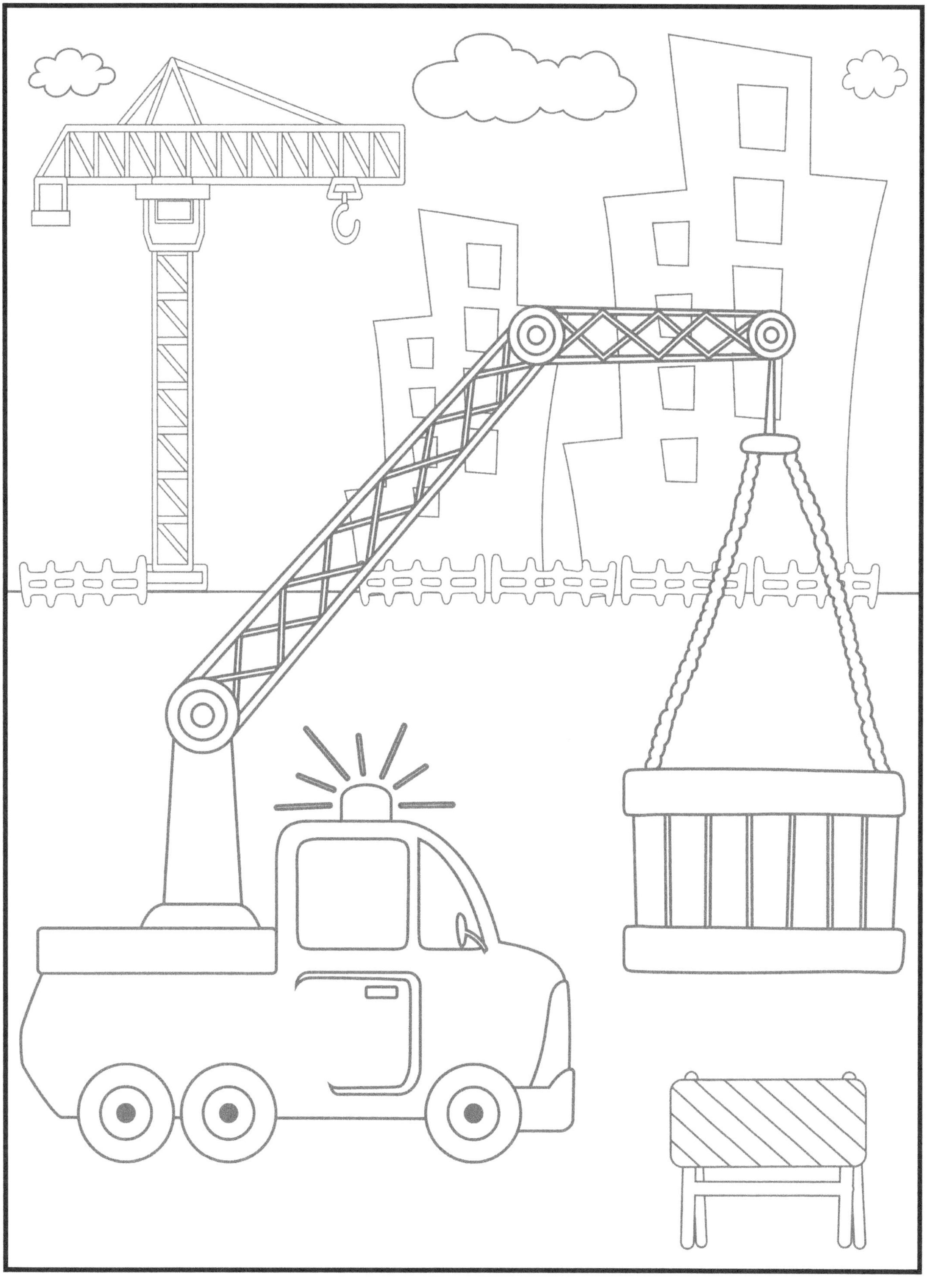

www.ingramcontent.com/pod-product-compliance
Lightning Source LLC
Chambersburg PA
CBHW081534220526
45467CB00010B/3181
* 9 7 9 8 7 1 5 6 8 9 1 1 5 *